The sheep statue that has become the symbol of Hatherleigh

CONTENTS

FOREWORD

It is a great privilege to be given the opportunity to write a foreword to Dennis Bater's wonderful book.

All of us country-born folk of a certain age will recognise Dennis' childhood - a Devonshire world not rich materially but one abounding with a deep sense of community; one which produced 'characters' whose idiosyncrasies linger long in the memory.

With his vivid prose Dennis brings such folk to life and illustrates how, so often, the strength of village life exceeds the sum of its parts; how all the strong, the delicate, the wise - even the feckless - play a role in creating a vibrant community.

A further strength of this book is that it is devoid of sentiment. Dennis describes his life - and the way of Hatherleigh and the area - over the decades, telling how it was and how it is. No 'things ain't what it used to be' nostalgia; no judgments passed; no complaints made.

This is a chronicle which, in years to come, students of social - and local - history will look upon as an essential reference book, while folks of today will enjoy it as a fascinating record of the life, so far, of an exceedingly interesting and accomplished countryman and the community in which he has lived.

A fascinating read.

TED SHERRELL

PREAMBLE

The book you are about to read is my account of the way I saw Hatherleigh and the neighbouring village of Iddesleigh as I grew up. I tell of my own experiences, and those of others that I have been told about and which, to the best of my knowledge, are true. I had originally compiled this book to bring the story of Hatherleigh - published when I was Town Mayor first in 1981 - up to the close of the 20th century. However, now in 2008 I find so much has happened over the last few years that I have decided to extend it.

I recommend some books that should be read in conjunction with mine, to get more depth of understanding to some of the events I have included. In particular, Reverend Banks', a Vicar who was interested in local history, did a great deal of research in the eighteen seventies and eighties. His researches record many events that townsfolk from Hatherleigh have stretched out across the world and, somewhere, have made impressions of some kind.

I have possession of a book of Parish magazines through the kindness of John Watkins (pictured right) who purchased it in Barnstaple Market and lent it to me on several occasions. One day he said that I should keep it as it might get lost when he died. Sadly he died barely twelve months later! Reading it inspired me to get to work and record my own memoirs.

I also want to thank the following people for their assistance and advice, and for lending photographs from their collections: Brian Abel, Hatherleigh History Society, George Dunn, Eric Rowe, Derek Coysh, Peter Fishleigh, Alan Jones, the Miller Twins (Mrs. B Heaman and Mrs. D Ball), Morris Thomas and G Andrews (NDJ, for cover photo).

Dennis Bater

THE BEGINNING, NATURALLY!

Week Moor Cross, and the cottage where I was born.

My father Fred Bater married my mother Violet Dennis in 1938 - hence I was named Dennis Bater. Fred had been a farm worker all his life; his wage at the time of their marriage was 35 shillings a week (mother told me her wedding reception food cost thirty shillings!). They rented a small cottage at Week Moor Cross so I started life in very humble beginnings.

My mother wanted me to become a car mechanic, but I would not be told and went on to become a farm worker! I had my way and later became, at various times, a lorry driver, the owner of a Fish and Chip Shop, a Postman, a Fireman, an amateur film maker and a school Governor. I also worked in Hatherleigh Market for some 30 years, where I was involved in collecting stall rents, building work, security work, controlling traffic and other odd jobs such as driving a digger, clerking and, once, helping bailiffs! This experience has helped me (I hope) to become an understanding Councillor who enjoys being able to help and steer the community I live in.

A garden was an essential and my father Fred was a keen vegetable gardener.

I was born on May 1st 1940 at Week Moor Cross - the house on the cross roads with the post box in the wall. My first memories are of playing in the well-kept garden in front of the house. In those days, from what I saw as a two year old child looking out from the garden gate, it seemed to me that the whole world passed by. I think the cross roads were busier in those days than they are today.

One early memory was the lady who passed by five days a week. She was called Mrs. McDermott and she taught at Iddesleigh School. She would cycle every day from Hatherleigh in all weathers, wearing a black gabardine Macintosh and head scarf.

6

My mother was in service working for the
Reverend Paramore before she married my
father. Rectories in those days employed
gardeners, farm workers, cooks and chamber
maids, of which my mother was one. It was
a standing order that all staff had to attend
church every Sunday morning. Parson
Paramore was noted for his long sermons and
after they had been written they would be laid
out on his desk in his study. So, mother's orders
on a Saturday from the other staff was to spy
on his Sermon.

*Myself at 18 months old standing
in front of the cottage.*

She would count the pages and pick out points
so that when they all sat in church the following day they could see how much
was left and when the sermon was coming to an end. His youngest daughter
Dorothy, who spent a lot of time with the staff, would also want the information!
The Reverend Nick McKinnel, in paying tribute to mother at her funeral,
remarked on this and the many tales she told him of her past service in
Iddesleigh rectory.

Considering that the farm worker's weekly wage was then only some four
pounds it must have been hard for my parents as, from 1943, we had holidays
in Dartmouth. My early memories of these holidays are of D-day equipment
covering the New Ground
and Quay!

*My Mother and Father with Janet my
youngest sister in 1966 at Dartmouth with
Lesley (second right) whom I would marry.*

*Mum in her
uniform.*

HATHERLEIGH TRIVIA – 1

SOME OF THE CHARACTERS

Hatherleigh has had an influence on all the parishes that it bordered. People relied on the town for most of their services. Deliveries came out from the town most days - delivered by characters such as John Edwards the baker, Burt Goss the butcher, groceries from Sam Ellacott who had his shop in South Street at what is now called Cobweb, and Wilfred Jerwood who had his shop at the Market and High Street junction. The fishman however came from Exeter. He was called Wally Rice. I believe that he was well known in that city, running a stall in Exeter Pannier Market and later a shop in Burnt House Lane. Coal came from Letherens (who traded until the mid-nineties and are now known as Cornwall Farmers), and also from Victor Brooks. He would also bring Sam Ellacott's groceries on another day of the week; on the same lorry he would carry paraffin and the odd few bags of coal he had missed on previous rounds, all covered by a sheet.

Football Club members. Mrs. MacDermott is front row right, left of Mr. E Pillivant, Hon Secretary. (Back Two Rows). J Reynolds, B Balsdon, ?, E Rowe,?, G Short, R Alford?, (Man Standing right at Back) E Pillivant jnr, Mrs E Pillivant jnr, A Edwards, R Short, J Westlake, Mrs J Westlake, ?, E W Johns, D Edwards.(Front Row) ?, G Hands, H Watts, ?, ?.

Sam Ellacott and daughter Gladys.

Victor Brooks in his coalyard.

Burt Goss and John Edwards were drinking pals who always met at the Duke of York, Iddesleigh, on Friday evenings after the rounds were over.

MY WAR YEARS

Ray Caton still visits now in 2007.

During the war my parents took in an evacuee called Ray Caton. He was not with us very long because my sister Ruth was about to be born and, as he was soon fifteen years old, he had to return to London.

At the time Ray was with us he had already endured several air raids at home, and just to hear the German planes over head made him panic and want to go to the toilet. In the countryside of course this was a bucket at the bottom of the garden. Many nights my father would be waiting outside the small shed for Ray, as he was scared of the dark. My father said that, as he waited, he would often see the flashes on the horizon of the bombing raids in Plymouth, although this is difficult to imagine now. Ray, by the way, went on to join the Merchant Navy!

A weekly treat in those days was for my Mother and Aunt Winnie to take my sister Ruth, cousin Tony and myself and walk to Hatherleigh, some three miles away, with the prams for shopping, passing the William Morris Monument on the way. I can just remember sitting on the bottom of the pram when we were coming home after dark on a winter evening. Crossing Hatherleigh moor, the raids in Plymouth had already started and searchlights were visible. This put the fear of God in me and I would crawl up under the hood with my baby sister. Wartime activity appeared to me as the normal everyday life that I was born into, so I do have some understanding of what it must be like for young children in war zones today, although we were of course in no way as bad as some troubled countries today.

Jimmy Thorne (see next page) was our next evacuee – he also came from Battersea. Both he and Ray have visited in later years. When the war ended I remember saying to my mother, who listened intently to every news broadcast on the radio: "Won't there be any more news on the radio now war has ended?" From the reaction of my parents at every news bulletin I knew that this war was something terrible.

HATHERLEIGH TRIVIA – 2

OF SCHOOL, EVACUEES AND NUMBER PLATES

The parishes of Hatherleigh, Winkleigh, Monkokehampton, Exbourne, Iddesleigh, Meeth and Dolton were made up of people who had lived in these places for generations, and it was not until the nineteen sixties that there were many changes. Fortunately, Beaford Arts photographer James Ravilious captured some of the characters before they disappeared and his books are a 'must' for country lovers. I had the pleasure of meeting him on many occasions and his photographs, which are now held by the Beaford Centre, are unique. When I was a child, Nethercott House played a big part in the village, as the Hatherleigh Harriers Hunt was kennelled there. Hunting was what people did in the country and the anti-hunt campaign was rarely heard of! Things that stick in the mind? I remember Captain Budgett had a shooting brake that was always passing up and down, and farmer John Ward had an Austin Seven with the number CDV151. Number plates have always been something I recognised people by; present day numbers are so impersonal!

Waldons Cross School in 1946. (Back row)
R Richards, C Holwill, M Richards, ? Allen,
R Anstey, A Weeks. (Front Row) B Richards, C
Anstey, D Bater, D Sparry, R Wilson, R Bater (my
sister) and A Bater (my cousin).

Some of the 40 others who were evacuated from
Battersea ready to board the train to Iddesleigh from
Okehampton in 1940. Ray Caton and Jimmy Thorne
are both there somewhere.

Because we lived at Week Moor Cross where the post box was in the wall, the postman would call at our house for any parcel that may have been left. The postman at that time was Sam Inch. Many readers will recognise this name. After the war he made his part time job of cider-making into a full time activity and became one of the top cider manufacturers in the country. Inch's Cider was taken over in 1996 by Bulmers and closed down in late 1999, but the factory was opened again by a man who had worked with Sam all his life. It's now called Winkleigh Cider.

Jimmy Thorne (see previous page) came to see me in 2002 and now lives near Torrington.

During the war a Hunter Class minesweeper took the name HMS Hatherleigh, named after the local hunt - the Hatherleigh Harriers. It was later sold to the Greek Navy. Now, Nethercott House is used by the charity 'Farms For City Children' run by Michael Murpurgo the author. This School brings children out from the cities and they spend the week learning about living on the farm, feeding the animals, attending births and assisting with mucking out and other country matters. This is often a life changing experience for many of them, as it had been for the evacuees during the war.

When I reached the age of four we moved to Waldons Cross, half a mile east of Week Moor Cross. My father rented two fields at the back and ran a smallholding. The memories here are of aircraft appearing out from behind the trees at the top of the field. They were still climbing after taking off from the newly-built wartime airfield at Winkleigh. The shape of the Mosquitoes, Beaufighters and Hurricanes remain vivid

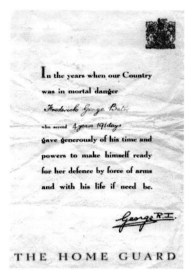

In the years when our Country was in mortal danger

Frederick George Bale

who served 4 years 191 days gave generously of his time and powers to make himself ready for her defence by force of arms and with his life if need be.

George R.I.

THE HOME GUARD

in my mind. It would be the 1990s before we would learn what had really gone on at RAF Winkleigh (read Ron Cottey's book 'The History of Winkleigh Air Field').

My father was in a reserved occupation on the land so he had to join the Home Guard. It meant that he had to go drilling at weekends and on the odd evening. The platoon often went off in Sid Hookways' coach to the rifle ranges at the bottom by Friars Hele Bridge on the A386 to practice. Hookways Pleasureways are now a well known name in the travel business.

At this time I started school and I hated it. On the first day I was dragged to school crying all the way by Jimmy Thorne and my cousin Arthur Weeks. Not a good way to start. I am glad the way schools are now set up with pre-school playgroups. This leads children into full time education a lot more easily. They have already made some friends and the change is so gradual that they are able to make a good start to the most important part of their life.

When I started school, who should teach me but the teacher I used to watch passing our gate on her bike when we lived at the Crossways. On my first day we were issued with blackboards and chalk and, until we could form our letters properly, we were not allowed pencil or paper. My friend was David Knight, commonly known (still is) as Shaver. His parents lived in a cottage at Nethercott House and his father helped look after the hounds and was often the driver of the shooting brake.

I remember Mrs MacDermott for another very good reason: I was reading to her at her desk one time when we came across the word 'said' which I did not recognize! She took me back one page and said: "What's that word, then?" I looked and said "said!" She took me forward one page and said: "Well, what's that then?" to which I said nothing. I got a big whack on the legs with her open hand for that, and it can be honestly said that I have never forgotten the word 'said' since!

It must have been 1946 when I first saw and tasted a banana. I saw Cissie Holwill (she

12

is second in the back row in the earlier Waldons Cross childrens' group photo) eating one. I knew immediately that it was a banana because we had been told what they looked like.

We still had deliveries from Hatherleigh, but now at Waldons we had other bakers - Guys from Exbourne (delivered by Leslie Martin) and Cottles from Chumleigh. Another memory was the men in uniform calling for eggs and milk because we now kept two cows, a couple of pigs and some chickens. These were RAF personnel from the Searchlight Battery which was based about one mile up the road near Pixton Farm.

Food was short at this time for everyone but it has since become clear to me that people living in the country fared better than city dwellers. We had food all around us; rabbit stew was a favourite for most, although I hated it.

We often had a meal that I did like, and it is still one of my favourite dishes - salmon! My father's job often meant he worked near the river bank. The river was thick with fish in those days, also otters. Now otters love salmon and they would often catch one and pull it out on the bank, causing quite a lot of splashing. Father would hear this, drive off the otter and take the salmon home for supper!

Another memory was the Devon County Council lineman who kept his strip of road in good repair. His name was Bert Crocker from Monkokehampton. Often he would pass by pushing his wheelbarrow with some gravel in it and a bucket of tar swinging from the handle. His job was to fill the smallest hole as soon as it appeared. Please note that 'a stitch in time' in this case is particularly good policy, though if it was a bigger job the Council would come along with a steam roller. (I have to research this roller a bit more as it's possible that it is the converted steam engine that Fred Dibnah used in his final TV programmes.)

A family of Gypsy travellers lived around the corner from our house. They lived in a tent made out of lorry covers and were called Sanders. There was a lad, Michael, who was about my age. He would stand at the door wanting me to come out to play. I was never allowed out. I met a member of his family years later who told me that Michael had been a fairground boxer for a time.

As a child, I watched many characters passing our house by on their way to the Swan Inn at Monkokehampton. This was the only entertainment, other than the Duke of York at Iddesleigh! One of them was Tom Anstey. He was a sheep shearer and he would also contract out his labour to farmers for thrashing and combing reed. He also ran a smallholding near Bullhead Farm with his wife Loveday and a nephew Derek Coysh.

Tom's two brothers and a sister lived at Monument House on Hatherleigh Moor. One brother, Bill, was a thatcher but worked on Hatherleigh Moor with the War Agriculture Ministry (known as War Ag) for a time. Bert, his brother, was the lineman for the road from Hatherleigh to Iddesleigh. Ernie Woodrow was one of Tom's friends - he lost his arm in a chaff cutter and had it replaced with a crook - and together with Simon Brooks, and sometimes Lambert Brooks, they would be Tom's companions. All would come home from the pub holding each other up! Simon Brooks was our neighbour and one of my memories of him was carrying the water from the well 200 yards to his house in two buckets, using a yoke on his shoulders.

I must mention Mr. Hicks, or Hicksey as he was known. He suffered from shell shock after the First World War. (It took until the turn of this century before this particular illness would be recognised). He owned a bicycle which did not have a

Tom Anstey, and his sister Grace who lived in Monument House.

chain. His wife and daughter would push him up the hills. He then coasted down the other side and waited for them at the next hill. It was an unusual sight on summer evenings. They would go from near the airfield at Winkleigh all the way to Iddesleigh, via Fords Cleave to Monkokehampton and back around Iddesleigh to their home. Apparently, he compiled crossword puzzles for a national newspaper (possibly the Times). He was also rumoured to be an agent for Germany by the security forces at Winkleigh airfield and was watched very closely.

I don't think he was a spy but he would go and torment the airmen by standing at the bottom of the runway, shouting abuse. Apparently one day, having had enough of the insults, an airmen sitting in the cockpit of an aircraft discharged a cannon and the shells flew over his head. How different it must have been in those days. Today such endeavours would involve an inquiry.

He moved away not long after the war and went to live near Eggesford on the main Barnstaple road. He became a well-known figure to thousands of motorist travelling that stretch of road because he would be seen walking with his coat pulled over his head!

Simon Brooks, known for his quick marking at the Dart Board using his good ability at mental arithmetic.

Another character was the late Harold Glover, a man of great strength. He was a contractor and worked very hard ploughing the land for food in 1940. He has told me that he often kept his Allis Chalmers tractor going for days non-stop as he had difficulty starting it. He would just sleep for an hour by his tractor (engine still running) to refresh himself and go on again. To give you some idea of his strength, he once bet George Tucker, the Hatherleigh blacksmith, that he could carry his anvil the length of Market Street and back. Harold won the bet. George also told me that he once saw Harold load a binder on to a trailer all by himself. George, being highly impressed, told many other tales of this man's great strength.

After the war we continued to live at Waldons Cross. Two other things come to mind whilst we lived there. First, father would go to Hatherleigh on his bicycle to fetch fish & chips. When you consider this was a three and half mile cycle ride, some of the way up very steep hills, this was a real luxury. Secondly, we could hear the Hatherleigh fire siren when the wind was in the right direction.

Little did I know that one day both things would play a big part in my life!

HATHERLEIGH TRIVIA - 3

UFOs ...

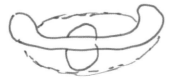

In the late sixties two police officers followed a mysterious object whilst patrolling the A3072 Holsworthy to Hatherleigh road. It led them onto the road to Bassett's Cross and then it disappeared. It was passed off by some as the planet Venus which was bright at the time, but Constable Ralph Wadie told me that the two constables were very down to earth and not easily confused. His leaning was towards something more sinister. The incident was featured on television and, more recently, on Sky TV. Another sighting was made by my own daughter and her friends in 1978, on a Sunday afternoon when they were playing hide and seek. They were about twelve years old and Beverly Reynolds was hiding behind the International Stores (now the Co-op) with her cousin. As my daughter Lisa was trying to find them they came out shouting that they were being watched by a strange thing in the sky. Lisa must have seen it but she had not been as near. As I went to fetch them for tea they were running up the road urging me to come and see. I saw nothing. They had obviously seen something out of the ordinary so I said the best thing was to go to their separate houses and draw it! (see sketch above). The astonishing thing was that all the drawings were similar! I know that they did not expect me to send them to do this and I did not give them time to connive the same drawing. They said it went off in the direction of East Dartmoor. The following week the local planning officer at Okehampton saw an object whilst walking on Belstone Common, though it was cigar shaped. Another sighting was by a bus driver at Friars Hele. As he returned home to Meeth he saw what looked like long white tubes in the sky. Flashes in the sky were reported by other people. Yet another sighting - near Dolton Beacon - by someone who does not want his name published - was of a bright light coming from behind a hedge. He peered over and saw a very bright sphere-like shape. It took off and he said he had never seen such speed as it disappeared. We await the next sightings.

... AND ROCKETS

In April 1998, a Scientist from Sheffield University came to Dartmoor to launch a rocket to the edge of space. Unfortunately it crashed on take off and set fire to the Moor, causing a lot of damage. I managed to take a photo, though not a very good one. Had the launch been a success we would have had a spectacular view.

I GROW UP

After some five years we moved to a cottage in Ash Lane about half a mile nearer to Hatherleigh. Here my sister Janet was born in 1950.

Iddesleigh School was to close that year and BBC television came to the area to make a documentary. Only a few of us knew what television was. I had seen a display at the Festival of Britain a couple of months before and had stood in wonder. My family were lucky to be invited to watch this programme by the owner of JVS, a radio and TV supplier in Okehampton. After the closure, the children were to go Winkleigh School until they were eleven years of age, and then on to Hatherleigh for further education.

Iddesleigh School just before its closure.
(Back row) D Squire, D Parker,
B Richards, S Alvis, J Farleigh.
(Mid Row) T Bater, C Ansty, V Parker,
V Vanstone, R Bater, T Farleigh. (Front
row) me, J Parker, P Alvis, T Squires.

When I arrived at Hatherleigh School at eleven years old, I made friends with children from villages I had never heard much of, such as Petrockstowe, Sheepwash, Highampton and Black Torrington. At that time, only six years after the war, children did not have the opportunity to travel.

My first teacher, Mrs. MacDermott, was now teaching at this school but she did not teach me. My teachers were to be, in this order, Mr. Jones, Mrs. Menzies, Mrs. Jones (no connection with the first Mr. Jones - she was Leonard Jones' wife, owner of the Garage), Mr. Wilcocks and Ernie Johns. The head was Mr. Brown. I happily left school at fifteen, with Ernie Johns' report to my parents that said: 'Dennis could probably play a good part in any community. He has a problem expressing himself on paper but he has a good memory'! It was about a year later that Hatherleigh School closed its doors as a Secondary Modern school and became a Primary School. I would go on to be a Governor later.

On leaving school, I went to work on a farm called Iddesleigh Mill owned by Tom Murrin. The very first job he gave me was to go and cut the docks in the field known as Mew Platt.

Tom Murrin in Hatherleigh market wearing breeches boots and leggings. Second left, standing on the rails, is Bill Yelland, my father's employer.

While I worked at the Mill, Hatherleigh was still the main town. For everyday needs, George Tucker came out to repair the implements. He would arrive in his old Trojan van, which was chain driven. He told me that when he first acquired the vehicle it had solid tyres. Tom Murrin's only transport was his bicycle, which he would ride to the market most weeks.

Another memory between 1955 and 1965 was the amount of air traffic over our area. During the daytime we had Gannet aircraft continually flying up to the old airfield at Winkleigh. Although they did not land, they would do dummy runs over the runway. On one occasion a tragic crash occurred killing all three of the crew. Add to this Vampires, Meteors and, later, Hawker Hunters, which would be constantly flying on training from Chivenor near Barnstaple, all at about 500 to 1,000 feet.

Making trails in the sky at about 30,000 feet were the B47s and, at 15,000 to 22,000 feet, Stratocruiser aircraft. We were on the flight path to the new Heathrow airport and fare-paying transport was now starting to become big business. There was no complaint about noise and yet the low flying traffic was much heavier than it is today.

The motor car was still out of reach for most of the young and when we went out at weekends it was by bicycle. We would go to Hatherleigh or Okehampton on Sunday evenings and we were continually troubled by PC North of Exbourne. He was a real lawman and we could tell you many stories about him! He was always around checking our cycle lights - which were often not working in those days - because being without a back light was breaking the law, big time. Some of the lads from Hatherleigh who had passed their driving test would borrow a car from Ian Norman.

Gannet.

Stratocruiser.

He ran the Garage with his father in Hole Court (until recently this was Hancock's garage).

Sometime in the late forties or early fifties an auctioneer called Joe Vick started to expand the existing cattle market. It grew rapidly and by the end of the decade was probably the most prosperous market in Devon.

Joe Vick, the founder of Hatherleigh market as it is in its present form.

Claremont housing estate was also being built about this time. Devon County Fire Service built the present fire station in the mid to late 1950s and, not long after, the station received a new appliance - a Bedford J4. Its registration number I can still recall - 999 LTA (see picture in Hatherleigh Fire Brigade chapter).

Around 1960 the concrete works were built by Woolaways of Barnstaple. The manager was Bill Reynolds. One of their drivers - Ivan Jones - worked there from the start and only retired in 1997. He sadly passed away in January 1999. The works closed and all was removed by December 2006.

When I reached the age of twenty-one I left the farm at Iddesleigh Mill. I wanted to see the world! In hindsight I should have listened to mother and been a mechanic!

Hatherleigh Market in its heyday.

21, and old enough to drive a lorry!

At 21 I was old enough to drive a lorry. There was no need for an HGV licence in those days - you just went out for a couple of days with another driver until you were considered ready (I went with Bill Spry)! I managed to hit a car! And who should come along but my mates Brian and Bruce Letheren! Bruce reminded me, at Brian's funeral which took place, sadly, just before this book went to print, what I said: "You're the last b****** I wanted to see."

I joined the firm of R J Harry at Follygate and stayed there for three years. I worked during the great blizzard of 1962-1963 and we were caught out in the snow. This storm is still talked about. I was in the Land Rover that was trapped behind the small lorry in the picture (see below). It would be three days before they were all dug out.

We abandoned them and walked back to the depot half a mile down the road. We held on to each other, unable to see anything or anyone in front of us and the blizzard was so intense it filled every open space in the vehicle, even under the bonnet (see picture left). The straw on the left of this picture is on the back of the lorry shown below.

It was during this time that Beaver (because of his moustache) Beven's house was demolished at the bottom of South Street and Bridge Street, and the gardens by the school entrance were put in their place - possibly one of the last jobs of the previously-mentioned steam roller as I saw it working there, driven by Jimmy Butt. Beaver was a character who is still often talked about. I remember an incident when we were sitting on the school bus going back to Iddesleigh. One of the children, Peter Fishleigh,

feeling safe in the bus, shouted out: "Hello Beaver." He came up to the door with a clenched fist and shouted in: "Laddie - do you want your eye put in a sling?"

The shop that he ran can be seen in many old photographs of the town, although I can only

20

remember him when he was in the small shop attached to the main building. That would have been on the school side of the present telephone box. One other thing that he is remembered for is the box of 'Gob Stoppers' he kept in the window. Often his cat would lie across the top and if you bought some he would put his hand under the cat to get them. The cat just would not get up!

He also had a small car that had some of its floorboards missing. He kept this car with his chickens in the hen house and he once had a hen sitting on a brood of eggs in the back seat. He

Beaver Beven's house and shop (centre), on the corner of South Street and Bridge Street, was demolished in 1961.

would go out as far as Meeth, just to deliver a quarter pound of tea. There was a tale that one of his hens had died on its perch and had fallen down onto the roof of his car; he did not see it and went off on his rounds with the hen still on the roof!

Another character that must be mentioned is Dick Weeks. Dick had bad sight but he was always around helping to run errands for Ian Norman and other shop keepers. Dick sadly drowned in the river Lew that runs along the bottom of Hatherleigh. This river also claimed the life of one of his relatives - Raynard Weeks. The river has claimed quite few lives during the town's history!

It was in the mid sixties that the Hatherleigh bypass was first put into the future policy plan of Devon County Council (but it would be thirty years before we would see its fruition.) By this time I had left R J Harry at Folly Gate and for the next twelve months worked for Maria Liquid Foods on the old Winkleigh Airfield, and then for a few months at Vellaford Farm with Eddie Arnold, one of my friends.

Dick Weeks was often seen at this stone in front of the George. The stone is still there! It was kept when alterations were made to the pavement as Dick spent so much time there.

In 1965, I went to work for Joe Vick who founded Hatherleigh Market. I found him and his family very good employers. Still, today, many staff

Partying in the George.

work for them until they retire. The firm always gave good Christmas parties too - here are staff enjoying themselves at the George Hotel one year!

It was about this time that Hatherleigh market took a downturn. Joe Vick had built an abattoir alongside, which was quite an asset for the town, and business appeared to be booming. Cattle would be sold in the market and the animals would then be moved next door for slaughter. But, shortly after its opening, Foot and Mouth disease was confirmed at Winkleigh (many cannot remember this outbreak). It was on a very small scale - unlike the 2001 outbreak - but the market was closed for several weeks and this threw the company into financial trouble. It was a great loss to the town as it took several years before things got going again, helped by 'Lionel Turner', as the momentum had been lost and Hatherleigh had lost a big chance. Joe Vick had been a champion for the town. He was running markets three days a week and there had been rumours of a possible airstrip being made at Little Wood Farm for foreign buyers to fly in straight to the market. Some thirty years later, BSE and Foot and Mouth have once again jeopardized markets and companies throughout the region. There always seem to be setbacks for Hatherleigh.

It was at this time in the mid 1960s that the Moor View Estate was enlarged (numbers 1 to 14 had been built in the 1920s) but now a new entrance was made and the extension was started. Not long afterwards, an entrance into fields on the opposite side of the road was made, owned by Ian Norman, but it would be several years before this became a successful industrial estate (see below). Now, in 2006, over a hundred people are employed there, many in units built by Ian and rented out. Some companies have boomed while others have moved on.

Moor View Estate.

In 1966, I married Lesley Gooding and came to live in Hatherleigh. A year later our daughter Lisa was born. In 1967, three weeks after Lisa was born, I joined the Fire Brigade. In 1970, Garry was born, and my family was completed in 1977 when Nicola arrived.

I first got involved with the Hatherleigh community when there was a request for permission to sell alcoholic drinks in the Town Hall. This caused great controversy and you would have thought that the devil himself was on our doorstep. It was after about a year of pressure and a change in the Town Hall committee that the community succeeded in altering the Constitution. I was soon to learn that Hatherleigh every so often seems to tear itself apart with squabbles. So now might be the point in the book to give some information on how I became involved in so many

I married and moved into Hatherleigh, and in 1972 started to run The Plaice Fish and Chip shop with my wife Lesley. Here are Lesley's mother Dorothy, Janet my sister, Lesley and myself, just weeks after we opened. We continued to run the shop until my wife's death in January 2004, when negotiations were already underway for its sale.

organisations over the years. From the Town Hall committee I progressed to the Town Council, which led to me being involved in many other committees - the Carnival, the School, the History Society and Moor Management, eventually being elected to the Borough Council in 1991.

In 1970, when Sid Doidge had been running the local Fish and Chip shop for many years, Doug Wilkins - the District Councillor at that time and manager of the newly built abattoir - decided that Bridge Street should be widened. That Fish and Chip shop (it's Cornucopia today) was purchased by Devon County Council and was to be demolished along with a couple of houses next door. My father-in-law said Fish and Chips was a good business and why didn't we use the old Constitutional Club - see picture next page - which was in his ownership, and open our own shop? We did just that! But before this came about the old International Stores building on the opposite side of the road to Cornucopia became unsafe and had to be pulled down. Thus, the road was automatically widened. Then Sid Doidge decided to close his business. Lesley and I opened our shop in 1972 and called it 'The Plaice' (see next page), and we ran it for 32 years and made many friends. We sold the franchise to Charlie Entwhistle in 2004.

Lisa, my eldest daughter with Peter her husband (both far right), the night before they flew to New Zealand. They now live in Perth, Australia, with their four children. Peter's parents Maureen and Graham Kerr are centre front, with me and Lesley second and third from top left. My son Garry is far left with his wife Louise. Nicola, my other daughter, and Steve her husband are on my left.

But back to the story. In the late 1970s, Glascott Close was added to Moor View and it would be another ten years before Veal, along with Mayne and Morris Close, would be built. In 1997, Pearce's Close was started and the first houses were occupied in June 1998. The properties in South Street were also under construction at this time. I had become a Councillor on West Devon Borough Council on the planning committee, so I was involved in many applications after 1991.

*'The Plaice' in Bridge Street,
our Fish and Chip shop. It was previously
the Constitutional Club.*

*Lesley, my late wife, leaning against the
baker's shop in Bridge Street.*

24

I JOIN THE FIRE BRIGADE

The Fire Brigade is first recorded in the first ever Parish Council minutes where there is a report on the condition of the hoses and buckets. The first recorded fire I have found in my research is the burning down of Littlewood Farm in 1783. Several mentions of large fires in the town later include Vogwells, the George Hotel, the Bridge Inn and the New Inn.

The first Fire engine for the town was purchased in 1809 and used until 1923.

I joined the fire Brigade in 1967. In those days you had a medical and one night's training and you

L to R: sitting in the cab S Hooper, D Sanders and A Sanders.

were sent out to fight fires! Today you must go through many hours of training and pass a test to see if you are fit to go to a fire. I remember the first Thursday's training that I attended. The Sub-officer Sid Hooper taught me to run the hose pipe and to hold a hose. He said that would be the most important thing to start with as I might be wanted in the crew shortly. Little did I know that it would be the next day!

At 1pm there was a tremendous thunderstorm and off went the siren: lightning had struck Friars Hele farm house. This was the first house fire I had ever seen, let alone be involved in. I think it was a good start to go in at the deep end. I have found myself several times since starting things in a similar way! Another memorable fire was Dunsland House, which was about the fourth fire I had been to.

(Back row, standing) S Meardon, D Wicket, E Sanders, C White, A Sanders. (Front row, seated and standing) S Hooper, G Horn, Stn Officer K Pack, F Newcombe.

I attended many incidents during my twenty-seven years service. I have lost count of the number of road accidents during that time, also the fatalities,

HATHERLEIGH TRIVIA - 4

Foot and Mouth struck in a small way in the late 1960s and I left the employment of the Market because it closed for some weeks. I went to work for Avery's, the builders at Okehampton, who had military contracts at Okehampton and Plasterdown Army camps. During that time I worked at Plasterdown, a camp that hit world headlines on three occasions and involved work for us in different ways.

The Northern Ireland 'troubles' were starting and troops from 60 Squadron of the Royal Corps of Transport - who were on 48 hours standby - were sent. Within days the troops were getting stones thrown at them and these were penetrating the canvas sides of their Land Rovers, so I helped two carpenters to fit plywood linings to the next lot of vehicles to be sent. (Some difference to how these vehicles would to be fitted out by the end of the Troubles).

The next came after the troops had moved to Catterick in Yorkshire. There was trouble in Malta and Mr Mintof kicked out 40 Commando within weeks. They came to Plasterdown which was a camp for emergency use. It was not long before 40 Commando would move on to Taunton, where they still are.

During all this time, I would meet people that I would hear of or come in contact with again, one being the present Tavistock Town Crier - Bob Rose - who was a Sergeant Major with the Medical Corps. There was also a USA Captain on exchange who would later be killed in Vietnam, and a Marian who would end up as an instructor in the Devon Fire Brigade and take a course I was on in Plympton! There was also a Sergeant who would die in the SAS helicopter crash in the Falklands.

Next to arrive were the Ugandan Asians, this time thrown out by Idi Amin, the famous last king of Scotland! We had to prepare the camp to take in families totalling some 800 people, a large number. And what a fool he was to get rid of them - the cream of his country! I met one again by accident later at a Royal Garden party and he told me he had returned to Uganda but had decided to live back in the UK. Another I saw on TV had gone to live in Plymouth and become a bus driver.

Finally, Mr Watts, who I mentioned at the start of the Book, met an Asian on a flight back from Australia, who told him he had been at Plasterdown as a child and was now a geologist! It's a small world isn't it?

A CLOSE SHAVE FOR NOEL

During the 2001 Foot and Mouth outbreak I organised a stunt with Jackie Kabler of GMTV. With the help of Gordon Reynolds we arranged with Noel Edmonds to film his early morning beard-shaving to raise money for beleaguered farmers. It was performed with a cut throat razor by Jo Barratt!

but I do remember two incidents in particular, which I had the misfortune to attend. One involved a cousin, Peter Bennett, whom I had grown up with and the other a child who had become entangled in farm machinery.

Left to right: G Coyse, C White, G Sanders S Meardon, E Sanders, A Sanders, G Horn, D Sanders, S Hooper.

Farms hold many dangers and account for a lot of our countryside accidents. They also accounted for some of the worst fatalities we attended. One incident which I feel is worth describing in detail actually had a happy ending. I was in the last two years of my service. It was the next night after Boxing Day in 1994, at about 7.30 pm in the evening, when we received a call that some sheep had been cut off by flood water. It had been raining all day.

We turned out to a field just south of Highampton on the Black Torrington road, where we were met by the farmer's mother. She was on a quad bike and she informed us that the sheep were in a flooded field some quarter of a mile away. I and the other Leading Fireman set off with her on the bike, leaving the rest of the crew with Assistant Divisional Officer Lane on foot. We had not gone far when we were called back. A message had come over the radio that two persons were trapped in a car that was being swept down the river just a few hundred yards up stream. So we doubled back and told the farmer we would be returning shortly.

Within five minutes we were at the car scene. A husband and his wife were indeed trapped in their car and it was being swept along the bank by the pressure of the water. We walked in above our knees to get to them, pulled them out and wrapped them in blankets; they were then taken to a nearby house.

An accident at the Price of Peace at the north end of Hatherleigh bypass. The two firemen on the left are D Moss and G Bater, my son.

Meanwhile, the Okehampton appliance had been alerted, but as we were now free to attend to the sheep it was stood down and we returned to the field and proceeded. To our left was a continual roar of water. We walked across two fields and came to where the sheep were trapped. We now met up with a river warden and he guided us on.

The old Milk factory at Torrington. Repairs can still be seen in 2006!

He warned us that on no account were we to go to the left as, in the darkness, we could walk into the river without warning.

The water was up to our armpits at some points and then just up to our knees elsewhere. We could see the sheep but it was clear nothing could be done without more help. By now our local RSPCA Inspector had arrived with some of his colleagues. We were told that the river authority would be attending with a couple of boats, but that would take two more hours so we decided to return to Hatherleigh fire station to dry out.

At about nine o'clock we set out again taking two extra firemen with us, one being my son Garry who put on a wet suit. We arrived back at the scene taking a different path. The boat had not arrived so we went down to the river to assess the best route to take. When they did arrive the boats were dragged over hedges and we made our way across the fields to the sheep. Lighting had been sent from Exeter, and Daniel Moss and a fireman from the Holsworthy crew, who by now had also joined us, set up the lights on a hill overlooking the area. We could just make out the island in the darkness some two hundred yards away but it meant going into four feet of water on each trip to rescue just one sheep at a time. Note in this picture the RSPCA are wearing life jackets, but Fireman G Bater has none!

By now, more men had arrived from the water authority, and the RSPCA! The Brigade's main concern was the number of personnel that were on the scene and to keep a check on them. One step in the wrong direction and someone could be lost.

When we were on the island all personnel were told not to go off the far end as this was very close to the river. We were soon to find out how near. We had plenty of manpower now so I took the photo below and was returning with one of the boats

when I heard on one of the personal radios that someone was in the river. This was one of my worst fears since I knew that in a river in that state it is unlikely anyone could survive. One sheep had run off the island and the RSPCA officer

28

had followed into the forbidden area, despite being called back. He may not have heard the shout above the noise of the flood water and consequently went straight into the river. A fireman, Steve Forrester (see group photos), seeing him floating nearby, reached out to grab him and fell in himself. He went down under the muddy water but luck was on his side and he came up by some bushes and held on. He was pulled out by a Holsworthy crewman.

A house fire to rear at Langham Chapel near Dolton.

The RSPCA Inspector drifted out to the middle of the torrent but luck was also on his side. He got trapped in between two trees. We could just see him in the light from our torches. Now there was only one way to rescue him and that was to call out the RAF Helicopter from Chivenor.

We then took the decision to drive the remaining sheep through the flood in the hope that we could save as many of them as possible. All went well until we came to the deep point. The current was quite strong and about four feet deep. The flock of sheep began to split up and all we could do was grab a couple of the nearest and pull them through. We then got back to the area where the water was about two feet deep. All we could do was regroup, have a head count and wait until help came. It seemed endless.

Eventually we heard the engine noise of the helicopter. It took some time before the crew could locate the victim with their heat-seeking equipment. This involved a difficult manoeuvre - the winch man had to climb down the tree (top to bottom) and take his rope clear of the branches. At the bottom, he coupled on to the victim and then both were swung out like a pendulum and winched up.

On the corner near the Holsworthy recycling depot, after freeing one of Gregory's lorry drivers.

After we had 'picked up' and returned to the fire appliance our crew members who had tried to rescue the officer were now very cold and wrapped in blankets. They had not been aware

Left to right, back row: S Forrister, K Drew, M Jarvis, J Keets, G Brooks, G Bater, (my son), D Tilly. Front row: D Bater, D Moss, A Cranleigh, T Reynolds.

Firemen off duty at a charity football match at the School
All these men are also in the picture above.

that the officer had been rescued, as the appliances were so far from the incident. We then realised that we were so lucky that we had not lost any lives for the sake of sheep who did not seem to want to be saved.

At Exbourne, at the bottom of the hill after the garage.

There are many other stories I could tell and I am sure all firemen could write a book about their own exploits. The following Story of Dunsland House is covered in more detail in the book 'Vanished Houses of North Devon', which is an accurate record and very good reading. Here is my memory of the incident. The building was owned by the National Trust and was a great loss to the nation when it burned down. On that night - the 18th of November 1967 - I had been serving in the Fire service for about seven months. At about 12.30 am the house bells rang (fire bells were connected to our houses by a telephone land line as the siren would not go after 11.00pm) and, as I ran through the door of the station followed by Derek Sanders, Sid Hooper came off the phone and said: "It's Dunsland House - well alight!"

Derek said that when we visited that house for drills we had been told of a well by the back wall so "we will have to use that for the water supply". As we got to the other side of Highampton we could see the house in the distance. It was the size of a match box but all the windows were picked out by the flames. The Holsworthy crew was already in attendance but the heat from the building just made it impossible to get anywhere near the well so we had to get water at the bottom of the drive from a stream. We set this up, and by now other appliances were arriving, but there was little we could do as by now the whole inside of the house was just one great fire - as can be imagined from the picture on Page 33.

I am the fireman coming down the ladder and Derek Sanders and Sid Hooper are at the bottom. What cannot be seen - on what was one of the most severe frosts of that year - is the ice that had formed from the water put on by the hoses, which was hanging in long icicles down from the walls as dawn broke.

As we were picking up our equipment to go home, a lorry arrived to do repairs to the house, with a ladder on board and a few slates. Some wit said: "You are going to

HATHERLEIGH TRIVIA - 5

THE POLICE STATION

The police have had a presence in the town since an order was granted at Sessions on the 12th October 1857. Before that policing would have been carried out by the Hatherleigh Moor Constable who was answerable to the Lord of the Manor. That post still exists. When the order was carried out in 1857 it was legislated that the town would have a station with two cells (see picture below, used today as a kitchen!), and quarters for a Sergeant, two Constables and a Petty Session Room. Every prisoner was granted a daily subsistence allowance of four pence. The station continued until it was closed in the late nineteen sixties. The town had only one Constable by this time, and I remember him. He was called Ralph Wade and he was transferred to South Devon, only to die shortly afterwards from a terminal illness. The cells have held one murderer - a man named Ware. (Read Chip Barber's book 'Murders in Devon'). Another police story concerns a riot which took place in Bridge Street. It involved the Sergeant standing alone against navvies from Plymouth who were employed in building the railway track. He fought with his back to the wall until the arrival of his Constable bearing extra truncheons, which were handed out to some residents. This story is recorded in a book called 'Out of the Blue' by Superintendent

Walter Hutchings, who was the Constable on that eventful night! In the early 1990's, a Police office opened up in Buddle Lane, in a small room provided for the Community Constable to meet residents in private. This was transferred to the market in August of 1997 but only lasted a couple of years. Today a Policeman or woman is a rare sight in the town.

HEALTH IN HATHERLEIGH

My first memory of a doctor was of Doctor Mitchell who was noted for making good medicines. The joke was that it came from two bottles, red or white! I caught the flu when I was about four years old but I was scared stiff of the Doctor. I started screaming as he came in the door and would not keep still. After several attempts to get near me he said to my mother: "The only way to deal with this young man is ... " and he put me across his knee and gave me a right tanning. I had never been given a hiding like that before and no Doctor has had trouble with me since! A hiding does work. I have never had any ill effects, but I can always remember it! I was told years after that he often made house calls on his horse after hunting. Doctor Mitchell eventually retire dthrough ill health and was followed by Doctor Kennedy, who later went on to practise in Harley Street. Then it was Doctor Wheeler for a short time, followed by Doctor McDowell, who moved his practice to Turnpike just around the corner. Doctor Pearson followed and at present we have Doctor Downey, who built the modern Surgery in Sanctuary Lane during the late 1980s.

Dunsland House - before, and after! That's me on the ladder!

need more slates than what you have there lad, to fix that!" The driver just stood there with his mouth open, staring at the shell that was left. Another vehicle then arrived to remove what had been salvaged. My memory tells me he was handed a vase and that was about it.

The exceptional drought of 1976 gave all Fire Brigades a busy time and often the crews were at full stretch with no extra men to draw on. Our station's entire strength was only 8! On one particular weekend we had a call at 9.00 am on Sunday to a hedge fire near Buckland Filleigh. After dealing with that, we were called on to two more hedge fires. As we finished with those (at about 1.30 pm) we had already heard over the radio that Westward Ho had a fire on the Downs, and that at the south end of the beach holiday makers were running into the sea to escape the flames. We were asked to attend. We said we were 'picking up' and, yes, we were on our way.

By the time we got there, most of the fire was out but we had to stay on to damp down until relief arrived. That turned out to be as dawn broke the next morning, by which time we had been on duty for 32 hours. At around 8.30 am - dirty and black - we were sent home.

In 1976 the river crossing at Passaford Bridge completely dried up.

We cleaned up the equipment but I had not even got back to my house when off went the siren again, and we were back to Buckland Filleigh and a plantation fire. This was burning like a mini-fire of the like seen recently on television scenes from California. It required 8 appliances and was important enough to bring the Chief Fire Officer

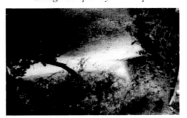

33

The Manor Inn, Ashwater.

of Devon to the scene. It was brought under control by about 6.30 pm. We made our way home. We had been without sleep for 48 hours and had worked all through, other than a couple of short breaks for food. I went home and got showered. Lesley cooked a big fry up which I ate in bed. It was now getting towards dusk. I said "goodnight," lay back and as my head hit the pillow, off went the siren again!

One young fireman, who I will not name, came in the door saying: "I cannot go on, I cannot go on!" He was quite distressed, so we sent him home. As I picked up the phone to take the message I said that it was now well over 48 hours since we had slept and could they find some other crew as we could be out for some time with no knowledge of when we would return. We had to go however, and headed for Torrington. As we got to Meeth a message came over the radio saying we could go home and get some sleep; they had found a replacement crew. The best news we could have heard!

We attended incidents varying from children locked in handcuffs, feet stuck in drain covers, chemical incidents and three air accidents. Although I missed photographing many of these these, I do have some nice photo records. One incident, a fire at the Manor Inn, Ashwater (see above), was reported by a pilot flying low in a jet fighter and

I received my 25-year long-service medal in 1992. Here it's being examined by Rod Lane. We also got a £500 bounty - but it was taxed of course!

he had seen an explosion. This is detailed in the book 'Fire and Rescue' by Sally Hollaway and Neil Wallington (Chief Fire Officer of Devon at that time).

Many times we had to work with other services - the Police, RSPCA and Coast Guards - but now, some ten years after I have retired, the Brigade works more closely with the Ambulance Service.

On the 1st May 1995 my twenty seven years of service ended on a quiet note - the last incident I attended was a false alarm with a smouldering garden fire at 14 South Street, Hatherleigh!

16 YEARS AS A BOROUGH COUNCILLOR

During the time I have represented the Borough, some residents will have approved of my achievements and others will have not! Some residents wanted a swimming pool and not a Community Centre. Financially, that would have been a big burden on the town, and the Borough, and impossible to achieve. Remember, as you are reading this, my priorities when serving have been housing, jobs and generally raising the lifestyles and standards for the area.

1998, the year I was Mayor of West Devon Borough Council, I gave a celebration for Parish Council Chairpersons at Burdon Grange. I am seen here with officers of the Council. Left to right: Lesley Smith, ?, Lesley Bater, David Incoll, me, Steven Gill, David Inman, Lesley Halton, Joan Thomas.

With regard to planning in particular it's impossible to please everyone all the time. The overall objective is to achieve a result that is lawful, economic, and beneficial. Sometimes, something or someone has had to suffer i.e. a loss of view or some building in the sightline, noise, dust and disruption to daily life but, after all this is taken into consideration, we can only hope for a successful application. SinceI joined the council so much has happened, and in the next few passages I hope to be able to enlighten you on some of the background, starting with the Industrial Estate.

Meeting Magnus Magnuson. I have also had the pleasure to meet many other well known people e.g. Jimmy Saville, Jenny Agutter, Shane Richie, Fred Dibnah, Acker Bilk, John Stapleton, Andrew Castle, Jackie Kabler, Richard Gainsford, Pam Ayres, many an MP and our local Radio and TV presenters, including of course Noel Edmonds.

Remember, a town can only prosper when there are entrepreneurs ready to 'have a go' and start a business. The part I play as a Councillor is to work with the planners to get projects moving as fast as possible, although many people do not understand that democracy moves slowly, which does present problems for someone trying to get started! Often funding for a project has a time limit and what with present legislation many projects fall at the first hurdle.

HATHERLEIGH TRIVIA - 6

THE RAILWAY, AND ITS POSSIBILITIES

The first train at Hatherleigh station ran in the mid-1920s. Standing on the platform on that day (left) was

Fred Gooding, second from right, (father of Wally Gooding - my father-in-law) who is also seen in the next picture (right). There he is hanging back trying to be the *last* passenger on the *last* train. Also in this picture is Mabel Westlake. However the last passenger was actually my cousin Peter Bennett who was noted for always being late! He ran across the track just as the train was about to go. I know ... because I took that photo! When I worked for Joe Vick he purchased all the rail lines and sleepers he could find. He stored them in the field where the bypass crosses near the Bowling Club and we worked for weeks stacking them. He made a good profit on the deal. But back to the railway; it brought some prosperity but perhaps the town could have done better. There were plans for a milk factory but, apparently, they failed to materialise because some farmers feared that wages would rise. Hatherleigh missed out again! And on a great deal more actually, because the original choice of route was from Paddington to Exeter, to Hatherleigh, and then down to Penzance. What of the town had this happened? It would have been put 'on the map', and with a milk factory would have been the biggest employer in the area, making the town a completely different place. Probably, we would now be the size of Okehampton. There were plans to build a branch line to Okehampton and work actually started on Hatherleigh Moor - a scar can be seen where digging started - but after only a few weeks this was abandoned. Plans are afoot to reopen the line to Holsworthy as a cycle track, going onto Bude via Holsworthy.

Negotiations for land have taken place and work has started in Church Road, Highampton.

BUT A DEATH TOO!

Not often talked about is a tragedy that happened at the time of the building of the railway. The track was transported to the town by steam lorry. One day, as they were parking up in the field where the filling station now stands, a length of track fell from a trailer and crushed to death a young lad called Jim Beven, the son of Beaver Beven! It was said that a woman saw the accident and grabbed hold of the track, bending it trying to lift it off the boy! In the picture, the gate where the girls are standing was where the incident took place.

THE INDUSTRIAL ESTATE

I mentioned elsewhere some of the things we missed out on as a town, but many have got going on the Hatherleigh Industrial estate, despite the challenges. Some have been successful, some have even moved on to somewhere larger. Some have failed. Did you know that there have been projects including Boat Building, Rocket Guiding Systems, Stationery Distribution, Plastic Moulding, Manufacturing Parts for Tractors, Kitchens, Motor Parts, Packaging and Distribution for major names like Woolworths and American Express, and the processing of frozen chickens?

What do we have there now? Pennon Group has a training site and also a storage area for South West Water; equestrian equipment is made and exported; Bones are a major pet food distribution company; Map Marketing makes educational materials and maps for businesses and schools; May Gurney designs and builds electronics for water pumping stations as well as servicing existing systems throughout southern England; Right Angle Powder coats metal and have had some interesting customers - there have been parts for the Hong Kong Airport Bridge, the elephant compound fence at Paignton Zoo, parts for the failed Pete Goss boat 'Philips Challenge', metal grills for the Bank of England and seats for Singapore Airport, to name just a few. There are also agriculture engineers, tyre fitters, car repairers, and storage. All in all, about 120 people work there.

HOUSING

Housing has been a great challenge. Which comes first housing or jobs? Now, at last, we have got the town boundary enlarged and the extra space has been taken up almost immediately, with Millwood moving in to start 100 homes. This is important because the school has falling numbers, giving concern to the Head and Governors, shops, pubs, and the post office. The needs of business to survive are extraordinary, believe me!

Beef event in Hatherleigh, 2006.

With the setting up of the new Primary Care Trust what of our medical needs? This could mean changes which might not always suit a small community like ours. Unless the town keeps going forward and growing, slowly we could fall back and lose some of the things we have come to expect for our everyday needs. This is something that has to be at the back of our minds at all times. These are very challenging times indeed.

37

Council business keeps me busy. Here, I'm signing the Waitrose contract during a charity cycle ride.

Now, building is under way on the new 60-bed residential home which we hope will bring, together with the re-opening of Burdon Grange at Highampton, another 150 jobs. So things are looking brighter. RGB Builders Merchants are already in the old concrete works (which closed at the end of 2005) and Lamisel Beams (we hope) will open a store somewhere in the Town soon. These are some of the achievements I have been able to help in some form or other.

RINGING PHONES

Other situations that have set my phone ringing (and my constantly being accosted in the street) have been: C-Far, the home for young offenders and adolescents, the smell in the town, the Rings Project at Moor View, and the Foot and Mouth burial pit at Meeth, which led to just one more threat to our abattoir. For many years it has been one thing after another with the abattoir. Apart from Foot and Mouth there has been a decline in livestock slaughter to thirty-month culls, and BSE and the banning of exports which was the main part of its business. All has come right in the end however, and it is still trading. Credit must be given to the late Joe Vick who built it. Now it's just one of a few left in the South West, although Foot and Mouth in 2007 is once again causing a downturn in farming.

When I undertook a charity cycle ride during my time as Mayor, the Waitrose contract had to be signed and submitted by the following Monday. So it was brought out to me when I stopped at a café on Davidstow Moor on the Sunday at about 10.30 am. This was the start of Waitrose at Okehampton.

THE COMMUNITY CENTRE

I remember at a meeting in the late 1980s held at Reed House and hosted by Major

The new Community Centre at Christmas 2005.

General Rougier, an appraisal of the town was being considered and Digby Greenhill made a remark that the old Town Hall was now sub-standard. I was more than surprised and thought that the Hall was very adequate but, on thinking about it for a couple of days, I realised

The Centre nearing completion in June 2006. The concrete works (left) closed at the end of 2005.

The hall in the Community Center, laid out for its opening performance.

he was right. We needed a new hall. I thought "what an immense struggle that will be to bring about". I had just seen Highampton achieving their new Hall and knew what hard work that had been for them. But some of us took it on and, after much fund-raising, on the 15th of September 2005 Stacey's of Holsworthy moved their diggers in and, by Christmas, things were well underway. The Centre was completed in September 2006.

THE BYPASS

I am sure that a visit by the Transport Minister John MacGregor in 1993 was the reason we got the go ahead from the Government to build a bypass. Given the severe financial restraints on our country since that time, I feel that had we not been given the go ahead at that stage the bypass certainly would not be there today.

Towards the end of 1993 there were signs that the bypass was at last going to be built and, in early 1994, diggers moved in to clear the trees so that birds could not nest. Three months later contractors Taylor Woodrow arrived and the road began to take shape. This was the first time Taylor Woodrow had worked for Devon County Council (DCC). The site engineer was Tim Baxter. Tim and I became very good friends and he did his best, together with Albert Walsh the manager for Taylor Woodrow, to run the operation as smoothly as possible, and indeed it was very successful. I met highways engineer Philps Turnbull (ex DCC) the day before the opening in 1995. He had passed the works to see how things were going and was pleased to think he had been in at the start. He

Before (viewed from west).

After (viewed from east).

told me it normally took thirty years for a plan to be realized. Philps sadly died later that year.

The bypass well under way ...

... though floods slowed things down!

A few weeks into the construction, the River Lew was to show the builders that they must 'have respect'; the river flooded three times in three weeks! The bridge was one of the first parts of the plan and yet it was the last to be finished.

By October 1995 the bypass was completed. It was opened by the Chairman of DCC, Councillor Westlake, and it was a great honour for me to stand on the podium for the opening, as I was the Town Mayor for that year. It had been the concern of many, not least myself, that the road would lead to the demise of the town and shops. Thank goodness my concerns were unfounded. Also, in 1996 we had an enhancement scheme, with new pavements, the electricity wires were buried underground in Bridge Street and the street lights were replaced.

MAYOR, FOR A SECOND TIME

In May 2007, it was a great honour for me when I was elected Mayor of West Devon Borough Council for the second time. In the position as Mayor, it's always a pleasure to meet people who work so hard to keep communities together and village services working. During my two terms I have visited on occasions - some times more than once - Lamerton, Brentor, Marytavy, Lewdown, Princetown, Horrabridge, Southzeal, Bridestowe, Bere, Alsdon, Highampton, North Tawton, Chagford, plus of course many trips to Tavistock and Okehampton.

One good reason for the bypass. This accident happened in Bridge Street only a few weeks before the bypass opened!

When visiting these places we often meet in village halls. I believe these are the most important buildings in a community now, what with the closures of post offices and even village pubs. These buildings will soon become the only place for the community to gather, perhaps even acting as community run shops and pubs? But they must be comfortable too. As Margaret Garton, one of our Councillors who is a stalwart

40

of the village hall, has stated many times: "If you go to a village hall in the 21st century it should be as welcoming and as comfortable as your own home; we must move on from the damp smelly cold buildings of the past". West Devon is making headway in achieving a good standard, but there is still some way to go.

Of course things do not always go as planned. Here are some things that have gone wrong:

- Tavistock Civic Dinner: I was Mayor in 1998/9 and the Mayor of West Devon is supposed to be the first one to be announced. Bob Rose, the Tavistock Crier, announced everyone else first, starting with the Tavistock Mayor. There was only Lesley and myself left so he came over and said: "Sir, what area are you from?" I said Mayor, West Devon! He realised his mistake and said: "Oh B******!

- The Carol Service at Princetown in 2007: I forgot my overcoat and the church had no heating - that was a bit of information I had missed on my instructions - and as we approached the church the temperature outside the car was minus two! Everyone else was wrapped up and they looked at me as if I was an alien. The minister taking the service took pity on me and lent me his jacket, as he was in his robes.

2007 was very busy and a couple of times I got my timings wrong, but we were always able to get a photo and, at the end, all looked well! When my year in office ends on May 20th 2008 it will have been a memorable time for me ... but it will be good to get my normal life back!

Devon is to consider being a Unitary Authority and this time it's more of an order than a Government request! It's been resisted many times but this time it looks certain to go ahead. I can tell you that, at this moment, no one knows of our future, or how important decisions will be made after 2011. I believe 'unitary' does not suit the shires. Unfortunately, democracy as we have known it is not now in fashion, and is disappearing. The community's needs in general are being moved further away from the decision makers and we will have little input in the future. This is not yet recognised by the man in the street and it will be regretted as we continue into the 21st century. When I meet my neighbouring District Chairmen and Mayors at events one realises that the people who serve in these positions are hard-working people and they are worried for the future of local Government and where power will come from.

HATHERLEIGH TRIIVIA - 7

REUSABLE ENERGY

Christies was a company that used gas from the old Gas Station to produce electricity. Their employees were Wally Gooding, my father in law, and Havelock Searle. As an apprentice was paid one penny an hour, Havelock once told someone that his first week's wages should have been 44 (old) pence, but that he got 48 that week because he had worked 2 hours overtime. I feel that these small energy plants will come back in

years to come. A survey was carried out in the town assessing reusable energy from animal manure in the early nineties. This technique is now to be used in other parts of the county. At that time, no one was prepared to finance the project, so Hatherleigh lost the opportunity to be in the front line. Holsworthy, however, formed a cooperative and has a plant up and running - although they have had problems. Should it ever come to pass that we do produce our own electricity, this will be going back to the time when Hatherleigh first produced electricity using its own power. Later, gas ceased to be used in the town and that's possibly the reason why Hatherleigh missed out on a National Gas grid system too.

OLD HOUSES AND STREETS

Hatherleigh has retained some of its houses with very little change since medieval times, including No 15 Bridge Street and White Hart in Market Street, also 45 Market Street and 43 Bridge Street. One that has not needed any restoration is Vine Cottage. The oldest streets are South Street, Red Lane, and High Street. One theory is that Buddle Lane was the main street in medieval times, which is a possibility as the houses that continue up Bridge Street from Buddle Lane are much newer. Was this the old 'Fore Street' perhaps? This could have been from the bottom of Buddle Lane to the junction of Market Street and High Street. Could Conduit Street, a name from the past, be the short stretch from the top of Buddle Lane to Market Street? We can only surmise. Other houses include Beven's House, Market House and Vivian's Stores. There was also a Coffin House (see right), so called because of its shape. It fell down in the early 1900s, according to 'The Story of Hatherleigh'. Today, such houses would be preserved, but at that time there was no money to repair them and they were not in a saleable condition.

THE SQUARE, THE MARKET AND THE PUBS

In earlier times the market was in the current Square next to a market building. Hand-in-Pen is an Anglo-Saxon name for a market, and we have a Hand-in-Pen hill on the Holsworthy road, just as you come off the new roundabout. Therefore, one must consider that the original market was there in earlier times.

(Looking down Market Street) This must be one of the first photos of the market area - note the George Hotel, little changed today.

In the Square used to be an old Market Building. An earlier original was burnt down and the replacement was the ugly building seen in the photos. This became obsolete at the end of the 1960s and was pulled down by the Town Council in the early 1970s. The site was then idle for two years before being converted to its present use as 'the Square', which caused an uproar. The stone walls were added in 1990. The Square has been a bone of contention for years, since some residents think it should have been a car park. But I could not support that as the Square is used for many community functions.

Research shows that there have been more than ten pubs in Hatherleigh, most in or near the Square (except for the Bridge Inn). Today, the town has just three pubs left - The George Hotel, the Bridge Inn and the Tally Ho.

(Looking up Market Street) The old Market Building is on the left.

Years ago, all the pubs brewed their own beer. At the turn of the twentieth century, beer was brought in by draymen. Things often go full circle and the Tally Ho (once the New Inn) can - and has - brewed some of its own beer too. In 1997 a home brew shop opened for a short time. This is now a popular hobby. The old name for this shop was the Salt Box. It would be nice to see the name reintroduced although at present the shop is empty.

Tuckers Machinery Works in Market Street was also a Brewery in the 1700s, before the arrival of the Tucker family.

The George is thought to have originally been the lodging house for the monks who built the Church. We often see photos in the past of stagecoaches outside the Bridge Inn and one can only assume that this must have been a staging point.

The Royal Oak closed in the 1960s and the Market Inn in the early 1990s. Originally it was called the London Inn and was, for a time, The Rodeo and then the Havelock Arms - named after its landlord Havelock Searle - before finally becoming the Market Inn.

The Bridge Inn has just been sold after being shut for a few months and is being renovated by its new owners.

SPOT THE STAR

An interest of mine over the years has been to keep a mental record of famous people who have visited the town, or at least those that I have heard about. My late wife Lesley said I was star struck! Hatherleigh has been in the spotlight many times and, on a few occasions, I have been instrumental in bringing this about and I thought that it was time these sightings were recorded. Quite a number of present day celebrities have been seen in the town. I once gave a talk at the History Society dinner on the subject of 'Spot the Star' and had a good response. Some stories were told that even I had not heard of previously.

Ron Bendle, filming on Hatherleigh Moor.

But, going back to earlier times, I read in the book by the Reverend Banks that a man by the name of Weston, a world famous walker, visited the town in the 1800s. Apparently he often made the headlines in those days for walking long distances. I once read, although I cannot remember where, that Sir Frances Drake preached at the old Hurle Bridge Chapel. Drake's father was a vicar and Hatherleigh was on the mariners' way to Bideford, making it quite feasible as the Chapel was situated on this route. However, it was demolished and the material used to build a private chapel at Reed, and this can be seen on the end wall of what is now Edenside House today.

Some famous rock musicians live nearby and have been to the town. Rolling Stone Ronnie Wood has stayed at the George Hotel. Noel Edmunds, who lived nearby until quite recently, was often a visitor. Michael Murpurgo, the author mentioned elsewhere, lives nearby and his brother Pieter has visited on many occasions. He is a well known producer with the BBC, producing 'The Stars at Night' and many 'Children in Need' programmes.

Ted Hughes was filmed in the George on the day he was appointed Poet Laureate. Other celebrities that have been seen are: Sir Jimmy Saville buying petrol at Jones' garage; Diana Rigg, dining in the George; Kate O'Mara (from the 'Dynasty' series and 'The Brothers') staying there overnight; Rolf Harris was seen in the paper shop;

HATHERLEIGH TRIVIA - 8

ART IN HATHERLEIGH

It was in July of 1996 that the sculpture of the sheep (left) was created by Roger Dean (right, with his proposal model)with money from West Devon Borough Council and European funding. It was a popular choice right from the start and I have heard no one complain to this day. Visitors are often seen posing for photos by the statue. The agreement was that the school children played a part in these art works and the tiles on the Co-op shop wall were created by them. Joining these were the Millennium Plaque and the display by the Vet's surgery in Buddle Lane. Both were designed and made by an artist who lived in the town, by the name of John Roberts. New seats were placed in the town depicting different aspects of the town's history. One seat depicts the Wool Trade, by the yarn of wool near the old wool sheds that were in the Square before the Old School was built. A second seat is by the river where the Walruses jump in on New Year's day for local charities.

ANIMAL HEADS IN THE SQUARE

I am often asked why there are two animal heads at the entrance to The Square. One is a Ram's Head, shown below, and the located nearby is a Bull's Head (right, below). When I was Mayor during the Foot and Mouth crisis of 2001, I was offered these statues by a local artist. I knew the suffering the town had gone through during that difficult time and I felt that it should not be forgotten. I gave many press interviews from the location and I felt that this was the right place to put the statues as a powerful reminder of that awful time.

Angela Rippon filmed here when she worked for Spotlight; John Gregson, famous for the film 'Genevieve', dined at the Bridge Inn; I saw John Craven in the Market; Acker Bilk came here to play in the Town Hall just as his recording 'Stranger on the Shore' was coming into the hit parade; Jimmy Edwards gave a lift to a resident who was hitchhiking back from Okehampton (he was on his way to buy horses at the same place as the Princess Royal); Wilfred Pickles and his wife Mabel (at the table) came to the town with his radio programme 'Have a Go'; Keith Chegwin filmed here for

Michael Burke, in the present market.

Channel Four's 'Live in the Morning' programme; I myself saw Prince Charles drive through the town one Saturday night when he was at Plymouth naval base.

The Princess Royal has made private visits for horse dealing. She spoke to Geoffrey Cleverdon when he was lucky enough to have been invited to a Royal garden party. She said: "Where do you come from?" He replied: "Mam, I come from Hatherleigh in Devon, but you would not have heard of this small market town." She said:"Yes, I have visited it on occasions when horse buying with my ex-husband Mark Philips." I have heard since two other stories concerning her visits. Prince Edward came on an official visit to present Duke of Edinburgh awards. In the 1950s Prince Philip passed through after a visit to North Devon.

At election times, big names that I have seen canvassing in the town are Ted Heath, Jo Grimond, David Owen, John MacGregor and Charles Kennedy. One person I had the privilege of listening to was Lord Tonypandy. He was a wonderful speaker and I was privileged to hear him at Emma Nicholson's and Sir Michael Cain's wedding reception in the Town Hall. Paddy Ashdown came, followed by the press including Michael Burke the newsreader, who seemed to be as popular as the MP! Another correspondent - Caroline Kerr - came on that day too.

Residents on radio in the days of Devon Air. (Back Row) Brian Letheren, Sarah England, Tim Laing, (Front Row) Geoffery Cleverdon C.B.E. Presenter Simon Pearce, Margaret Lock and Fay Kingsford. I took the picture.

Filming often goes on in the town. Ron Bendle, a local television presenter, makes short films on local events. We are grateful for the publicity. Some shots of 'The Recluse' were filmed here. The children's film 'Sam's Duck' was shot in the Market. At the close of the twentieth century, BBC 2 made a documentary on the present crisis in farming.

Other visitors included the late great Tony Hancock, who often stayed at The George. Kate Adie has reportedly stayed at The George too. She did work for a Plymouth television station at the start of her career. The author Ruth Rendell would call in on her way to Burdon Grange Nursing home to visit a friend. Joan Hickson would often come to see a friend who lived in The Square. Simon Bates has run a disco in the market and many cricketers have visited including Ian Botham, Tom Graveney and Jack Davy.

In the past, several famous wartime Battle of Britain officers have lived in the area. RAF aces include Brian Kingcome, Paddy Barthropp, Killer Kelly and John Killmartin. Visiting them were Douglas Bader and Johnny Johnson.

Finally, we must not forget Bill Oddie, Kate Humble and Simon King who, for the last three years, have filmed 'Springwatch' live at Fishleigh Farm. Terry Wogan has also broadcast his morning programme from Fishleigh.

The Foot and Mouth outbreak which struck the area in 2001 brought in media from all around the world. The British press included John Stapleton from GMTV, Andrew Castle, Jackie Kabler, and Richard Gainsford. I was interviewed by all four over that period, often in the Square - which is why we put the animals head sculptures there later. Some interviews were live, others were recorded.

One morning, GMTV's early morning programme was broadcast from the town. Pauline Quirk and Warren Clark have made a series in the area called 'Down to Earth' and the Square was used for on-site locations. Recently, Joanna Lumley stayed at The George and Dawn French at Thomas Roberts House, whilst filming a pilot series of 'Jam and Jerusalem'.

Recently I was in a local Taxi. The driver started his usual patter and happened to say: " I have delivered some famous people to Totleigh Barton near Hatherleigh, the centre for art and meditation. I took Jerry Hall and JK Rowling there." It would be interesting to know if some of Harry Potter was written there.

TWO WORLD WARS

1914-1918

During the First World War, men from Hatherleigh and the neighbouring villages volunteered. They accepted the King's shilling and were as keen to go as the next man. But casualties were heavy and many men lost their lives during the Battle of the Somme. Northlew, a neighbouring village, lost more lives per head of population than any other community in the country.

Farm horses were commandeered to be taken to France for the war effort. More can be read on this subject in Michael Murpurgo's book 'The War Horse', a book based on the village of Iddesleigh.

This photograph shows farmers from the Hatherleigh area bringing their horses to the market for collection, prior to being taken to the war front. This was called 'impressment'. The horse were graded by Army vets - either for light work or for pulling heavy guns. This photograph was taken in August 1914, and was described in the book 'The War Horse'.

1939-1945

The Home Guard, made famous by the series 'Dads Army', was not so far from the truth in Hatherleigh, as each week the local platoon had to drill and patrol. Some men had never fired a gun before, although many farmers were brought up with guns and were excellent shots.

Some tales I have heard are quite comical. My uncle, Tom Bater, was the trainee gunner in a Bren gun demonstration at the range. The instructor told them to gather round, there was nothing to fear! Unknown to him there was a live round in the Bren and when, during the demonstration, the trigger was pulled, the bullet shot out of the gun, thankfully missing all those troops standing around.

Mills Bombs were another hazard and there was many a scare at Hele Bridge

HATHERLEIGH TRIVIA - 9

COL WILLIAM MORRIS

On Hatherleigh Moor stands an obelisk, built by public subscription to commemorate Colonel William Morris who led the Charge of the Light Brigade in 1854. William Morris was born at Fishleigh Estate. He transferred to the 17th Lancers just before the Battle of Balaclava and is depicted leading the charge in the film 'The Charge of the Light Brigade'. Seriously injured, he was dragged off the battlefield by two Privates who won the Victoria Cross for their heroism. He continued to serve but died two years later in the Punjab in India. It is said that, had he returned to Hatherleigh, he intended to build a racecourse on Hatherleigh Moor. That would have been a wonderful opportunity. Could we have been another Uttoxeter or Newmarket? In September 1998, an author called John Dwyer from Texas stopped me and asked the way to Fishleigh Estate. He said he intended to write a book about William Morris and the Charge of the Light Brigade. If it is a best seller in the U.S.A. - like his present book Stonewall Jackson - it could encourage a string of Americans to visit William's birthplace. I have heard nothing since so perhaps he was not impressed. On the 25th October 2000, one hundred and forty six years on, Hatherleigh re-dedicated the monument. Members of the Queens Royal Lancers attended and their Colonel in Chief Lt. Gen Sir Richard Swinburn gave an address. Brian Abell of the History Society explained the history of the monument and I spoke about my childhood memories and the obelisk's future maintenance.

At the Obelisk on Hatherleigh Moor, Jim Reynolds blows the bugle taken from the dead bugler at the Charge of the Light Brigade.

COLONEL PEARSE

The Belvedere Tower is on the edge of the moor, quite near the William Morris obelisk. It was built by the Pearse family but it is unclear whether it was built by Col. Pearse, the crack shot who won the Queen's Prize at Bisley, or his father. Pearse was one of the people to introduce banking in the town. In the woods near the Belvedere were stone tables and seats, also placed there by the Pearse family. They were used for picnics in the summer but, alas, the last owner took them with him to his new home at Briony Hill, Iddesleigh. I understand they are still there.

Home Guard 1939 - 1945: (Back Row) W Davy, E Scammel, M Hannes.
(Second Row) E Pillivant, E Rowe, B Daniel, W Newcombe, E Sanders, J Mitchell, A Sanders. G Reynolds,
F Leverton, S Mayne, C Ball, T King, ? MacDermott. (Third Row) W Johns, W Fishleigh, A Palmer,
F Newcombe, H Cudmore, E Millar, R Westlake, H Luxton, P Cleverdon, C Pearse, L Jones, C Denford,
M Chick. (Front Row) B Miller, A King, D Miller, E Gloyn, G Vallance, L Crocker, W Collacott, M Sarson,
H Watts, H Goss, M Reynolds, R Newcombe, W Hocking, D Alford.

range, and elsewhere in the country, as the trainees dropped them through fear (demonstrated in one episode of Dad's Army). Apparently, on one occasion, the platoon split up and one group had to get in and attack a position in the town. They thought the best approach was to come down through the gardens of Market Street, which meant climbing through several lofts and sheds. One owner had onions stored in his loft, which they sent flying all over the place! They never confessed to the damage when he complained at the next week's training. He was playing the part of the enemy who they were attacking!

On another occasion a well known butcher came home one night from Okehampton Market, well oiled after a good day. Unknown to him, training had already started. This time the exercise was to build a barricade across the road by the Bridge Inn, using anything at hand - bits of cars and wheelbarrows - anything. The Sergeant remarked at the time: "Well done lads - that will stop any German tank!" Well, the butcher came around the corner, did not see the barricade and drove straight through it and on towards home, not feeling a thing. He proved that the Hatherleigh platoon could build barricades to stop tanks ... though not the local butcher! Apparently, he should have been on duty at the time and just escaped a court martial. I can imagine Private Pike saying: "Shoot him, Mr. Mainwaring, go on shoot him!" and Captain Mainwaring saying: "Stupid boy!"

HATHERLEGH TRIVIA - 10

CLIPPER YELLAND

A young man from Hatherleigh joined the Devon Police and some time later was posted to Dartmouth. When on patrol by the railway line at a point near the lower ferry he came across a group of midshipmen from the Naval College who were very much the worse for drink, and urinating across the railway line. He approached them and got some lip from one particular sailor, so he gave this midshipman a clip around the ear and sent them all on their way. He must have made a report. The sailor went on to become king of England (King George VI) and the King commented on the incident on a official visit to the college years later. The policeman (above) was born in South Sreet, in part of No. 32, and was from the Yelland family. He was always known as Clipper Yelland (although, was this from before the incident, or after?) This story came from the Western Morning News, and I have since heard from a member from the Yelland family who gave me newspaper cuttings to confirm it!

SCHOOLS IN HATHERLEIGH

The Rev Cradock Glasscott heard that a genius called Thomas Roberts lived at Clovelly. Roberts had designed the Hobby Drive - a very difficult piece of engineering by all accounts - in the 1800s. An approach was made and Thomas Roberts came to Hatherleigh to build a private school for boys in a burnt out house at the top of South Street called Eddys. He also made a pond on Hatherleigh Moor to teach his pupils navigation. In 1838, the National School was built in the Square on the site of one of the old market buildings, operating there for 38 years. In 1876, a larger school was built in the current location. Head Teachers recorded in the last century were Seldon, Sealy, Lane, Brown, Tucker, Holbrow, Zinideric, Barbara Shaw, Linda Mitchell and Caroline Boother.

TWINNING WITH BALLOTS

This picture shows the Fire Chief planting a tree with Monsieur LePage, the Mayor of Ballots. Hatherleigh has been twinned with Ballots, which is in the north west of France, for over 25 years. They are shown in a special

garden in Ballots dedicated to Hatherleigh and it was on the first official visit, the first time many Hatherleigh residents had ever been out of the United Kingdom. Friendships were made that exist today, though twinning numbers have dwindled.

Another favourite trick of the Monkokehampton platoon was, if the Sergeant did not give the 'right wheel' at a bend in the road, to march straight on up the hedge and down across the field, with the Sergeant running after them swearing.

When Dunkirk was evacuated, some troops were billeted under canvas in the field where the bypass now crosses next to the Bowling Green. I was told that some of the troops had left weapons lying around by the river bank because they had to move on so quickly. I remember, at school in the 1950s, hearing rumours that some children had found a revolver in a tunnel by the river near the fire station. I suppose it could have been one of the weapons left behind.

Just before D Day, American GIs were based on the football field. The Oxon and Bucks regiment were based on and around the Bowling Green field and also billeted throughout the town. The present Fish & Chip shop was their headquarters. The subscription rooms in Market Street were also used for administration. An evacuee's school was opened in the Old School, the Baptist church, and the sports field for a time.

What must get a mention is the house of ill repute which always seems to appear at any war time billeting. It was in the High Street area and it was said that customers would queue down Buddle Lane.

The sports field had roads made so that vehicles could go onto the pitch. After the war these were removed, and the stone used to make the track that now goes down to the gate at the bottom of Hatherleigh Moor near Deck Port Farm.

In the field just behind Oslo House there was a line of Nissan huts storing guns, ammunition and other army items. This was a 'no-go' area for the public. The Belvedere Tower was occupied by the Observer Corps. The officer in charge there was Capt. Budget.

The Observer Corps stayed on at the Belvedere until the late fifties. I joined them at the age of sixteen and stayed on with them until they moved to the top of Friars Hele Farm, where they had a nuclear underground shelter. The post at Hatherleigh was abandoned in the late sixties.

WOMEN PLAYED THEIR PART TOO!

The following is an account written by two local sisters - the Miller twins, now Betty Heaman (see right below) and Daisy Ball. They have kindly recorded their memoirs and I use their exact words here.

"Hatherleigh had its Home Guard section like many other towns and villages. It was made up from men exempt from service because of age or working on farms. Hatherleigh had eight women in their unit. At night some of the men would patrol the streets and their guardroom was at the back of the Post Office. Some of the unit would be transferred to the drill hall at Okehampton and would stay overnight and return at about six the next morning.

"They made the most of their spare time playing pranks on one another. When some were on guard in the guard room at the Post Office they could hear rats running over the beams and one member, a local farmer, opened the door and threw in a small stick and shouted: 'There goes a rat', causing pandemonium in the room.

"Sunday mornings were spent on the firing range. The women would go along to take messages on the field phone. Part of the range still exists today. It was not all duty - we had our entertainment too, with concerts and dance parties. Part of our entertainment was a brother and sister duo - Stanley and Freda Fishleigh - who were good singers. Freda went for an audition with Carl Levis, a BBC presenter of that time. Girls would sing with Kathleen Horn on the piano. Kathleen also played the accordion for the dancing in the Town Hall.

"There were Church parades on Sunday and a court martial if you had not attended guard duty. That was compulsory. Nicknames were common. One officer's wife was known as Sergeant Major Maud. The HQ was in a vacant house in Market Street and there we learnt Morse code and went to other sections using the field telephone. Sometimes the messages, when repeated back, were very funny as some part of the signal would be missed out. You had to keep your finger on the 'speak' trigger.

"But, all in all, we enjoyed our years in the force and, at the end of the war, we all paraded in the school playground and had our photos taken as we marched on to the church."

HATHERLEIGH CARNIVAL

The Carnival and the rolling of the tar barrels came together on the same day just after the turn of the century. The Carnival has not always been associated with the tar barrels, as it is today.

(1957) Bill Bowden on the tractor with Anne Cook, the Queen. Bill always purchased a new tractor for Carnival Day and drove the Queen's tableau.

When the first carnival took place, Ernie Pilivant, who lived into his nineties and passed away in 2000, was a very young child, dressed up and riding his decorated tricycle while being escorted by his mother. A collection was made for the Hospitals, which entitled people from Hatherleigh and Meeth to go for treatment as there was no NHS service at that time. This fund is still in existence and, occasionally, it gives to someone who is in need. Nowadays, it is usually used to pay for transport for hospital visits. The following year, more people dressed up and it became a procession.

There is no doubt in my mind, and in many others in the town, that the barrel legend is from the Gunpowder Plot. The Reverend Banks writes in the eighteen eighties that: "the young men are getting barrels ready to celebrate this old Popish plot", and this was incorporated some years later. The people of the town have always held strong views, as was shown more recently when, in 1990, there was a boycott of French goods.

The Carnival used to be held every November, usually on the nearest Wednesday to the 5th. In the late 1980s, this was changed because of a BBC TV show featuring Noel Edmonds and called the 'Late Late Breakfast Show', which went out on Saturday evenings. They wanted to do their weekly stunt live on Carnival Day but, in the end, it went somewhere else.

The Tar Barrel run at 5 am.

The Carnival never went back to Wednesday. Saturday has proved better as so many visitors and friends now come to stay for the weekend from all over the country, and even overseas A few diehards did not approve of this change and that caused a mini town split yet again!

This Willow Pattern float, constructed by the Gooding, Bater, Reynolds and Squire families, was built on an old caravan body and covered in clipped paper. (1978).

During the war Carnival was suspended, but on a couple of occasions a day of celebration replaced the Carnival, called 'Soldier Day'. After the war, in 1946, two Carnivals were held, one in June and the other in November.

To this day, the Pillivant family has connections with the Carnival and Louise Dilling, my daughter in-law and a descendent of the family, now sits on the Carnival committee, as does her sister and mother.

There has not been a break in the Pillivant family's involvement with the Carnival since it started in the early 1900s. Ernest Miller, also a family member and father of the Miller twins (see Home Guard section) took an active part in Carnivals.

The tar barrels have often been donated in the past. I heard that sometimes they were even stolen! However, for many years they have had to be purchased. In 2000, the cost was £50 per barrel. How much longer can we get barrels for this custom, and at what cost?

Lisa and Garry Bater in 1972.

This float poked fun at the Devon County Roads department because it took such a long time to finish the present Square. George Tucker and friends reckoned they could do better! (1971 or 1972).

TOWN SQUABBLES

I want to mention the squabbles that Hatherleigh has gone through. I have heard of many in the past, and some since I moved here in 1967. I have already said that people here have strong views and that these can boil over quite quickly.

After a bypass is completed, it is the usual policy of the County to spend some money to enhance the town. As most of the through traffic was removed everything was going fine until some of the shopkeepers felt that the widening of a section of pavement in Bridge Street down to the bottom Buddle Lane - some one hundred and thirty feet - would not allow traffic to stop and would therefore affect business.

Pressure was brought to bear on the Town Council to oppose the plan despite the fact that the Town Council had gone on a site visit some 18 months earlier with the planners and, at that time, had approved the plan to widen the pavement on this stretch of road.

I was a member on the Council but I had to declare a pecuniary interest as my wife and I owned the Fish and Chip shop that was alongside this particular stretch of pavement. Whichever I favoured, it would be seen as being to my personal advantage so I was on to a hiding to nothing. I was glad to see the project come to an end.

I really did not care which scheme was chosen but I was sad to see the way that people and the town were portrayed in the papers. This tended to tear the town apart. The bitterness lasted with some residents for a long time. Such squabbles can leave a scar in the town that takes many years to heal.

It's not the first time this has happened. I mentioned earlier the Milk Factory proposed for Hele Bridge. There was also the Chocolate Factory at the Station which caused a feud with a couple of landowners that is still remembered some ninety years later! It has often been claimed that, had these places been built, Hatherleigh would now be a much more prosperous place.

The Square was another big controversy. The Town Council again came in for some criticism so I will try to explain. The Town Council took out a loan to purchase the

BEATING THE BOUNDS

A tradition that continues to this day occurs every seven years with the 'Beating of the Bounds', which involves walking the boundary (or as near as you can get to it these days) of the Parish - a distance of about 7 miles, taking in fields, back gardens, woodlands, the Moor and even a house or two. Dozens of people participate, often returning from far flung places to take part in what they see as 'walking in the footsteps of my ancestors!' Even children take part ... many insisting on walking the entire distance! The Moor Management Committee took on the arrangements when it was formed. Refreshments are provided at intervals,

including hot pasties from local bakers. Various sub-traditions have grown up over the years. One takes place at Passaford Bridge where children wait in the river to catch coins thrown down by the adults, which creates lots of splashing! The five trees planted on top of the Moor celebrate the Millennium - one tree for every ten years since the Moor Management took over.

In 2000, a Boundary Stone was placed by Passaford Bridge, carved by Roland Edwards, starting another tradition - that the youngest would be 'bounced' here. The first two 'bouncees' were Tom Strawbridge and Jack Moyse, seen above left. Tom was bounced again during the 2007 'Beating of the Bounds', above right. Walkers start in Hole Court (below right in 2000) and the first challenge is to get into the churchyard which involves someone climbing a 12' wall! Other challenges include a house which now straddles the boundary and requires a small person to be passed through a window. Walkers traditionally stop on the Moor by the William Morris Monument for a group photo (below left) and refreshments.

Additional material and photos by Geoff Hodgkinson

site. They also had a grant to help, which is where the problem lay. The Council wanted to put in a car park but the County Council (they were the planning authority in those days and had given the grant and the loan) had a say as to what they wanted in the Square. They favoured an open space and, despite the views of a minority who favoured a car park, I think the County was right, as the Square is a good focal point for gatherings.

Another incident concerned the church spire, after it came crashing through the roof following the great storm of 1990 (see picture below). English Heritage agreed that it might be a good idea that the new spire should be lime washed, as it had been in earlier times. However, this was not thought to be a good idea by many residents. I think one of the objections was that there would be an ongoing cost for re-liming every few years, so the community felt that the oak shingles should be allowed to reach their former colour (a silvery grey) as soon as possible, which happened naturally within a year.

That squabble caused a lot of bad feelings and it did have a detrimental effect on the church, which I found very sad for all concerned It was a great pity that so many people were hurt and, had more time been given to mediate, this could perhaps have been avoided. I have discovered that many communities in Devon suffer similar problems over what often begins as a trivial matter. It is only pride that stops people getting around a table to find a compromise. I am sure these problems could often come to a satisfactory ending if they could.

In May 1998, a seat was having to be sited and again letters and petitions started coming in. A resting place was found under the Millennium plaque but two years later, after further complaints, it came to its final resting place 100 yards south of the filling station.

The Church Tower came crashing down in 1990 after the great storm.

More recently, concern grew about the new Community Centre planned for the 21st century, and again the rumblings of doubters were heard, though fortunately a town squabble was avoided.

At the end of 1999 the leaded windows in Old

HATHERLEIGH TRIVIA - 11

HATHERLEIGH MOOR

On the binder H Fishleigh, on the tractor M Crezberge

The Moor was ploughed up during the war because of the food shortage, growing mainly Barley, Wheat, Oats and Potatoes This was the first time that the land was ploughed. It was also almost the first time that tractors were seen in Devon in any numbers. They were mostly Standard Fordsons and Internationals, although a Caterpillar D2 was used for the first turning of the soil. It used a one furrow plough and it took George Stacey seven months to complete the job. Most of the machinery was imported from the USA and stored in a large shed between Monument House and Brooks Moor Head There was also another large shed down by the entrance to Mount Pleasant. The first time potatoes were planted, there was a first class crop. I suppose this was due to it having never been cultivated before. I remember the potato clamps dotted around the Moor and if my memory serves me right there were corn ricks around Mount Pleasant entrance. Jack Mitchell told me there were seven miles of ditches dug at the time the Moor was taken over by the war effort. Land Army girls were employed, together with Italian prisoners of war transported from their camp at Bridestowe. Later, convicts from Exeter prison were used. On one occasion a prisoner escaped. He was recaptured at Vellaford Cross after being free for one night. Bill Pemberthy was on his way home that night and, as he passed Vellaford, someone shouted. Bill did not stop but reported it to the police, and the prisoner was re-arrested when Bill returned with the Sergeant. He was sitting on the milk stand at the entrance to Vellaford Lane with a large stick in his hand. He confessed he wanted to steal Bill's bike. In the 1950s, the running of the Moor was transferred to the Moor Management Committee, on which I served in the 1990s.

HORSING ABOUT

One time, during my security work at the market, I was checking out sales tickets at a horse sale, to ensure payments had been made before a horse was taken and I watched the following incident unfold, from a distance. A youngish lady was selling her horse but was not going to see it sold to a dealer for meat, so she withheld it from the auction to enable her to chat to a buyer first and be reassured. A man eventually came forward who she felt she could trust so she did the deal but stayed on for a long time, sobbing and stroking the horse. The man came forward with his horse box, was cleared by me and then left with the horse, with the lady still crying and sobbing. In about ten minutes he came back and dropped the tail board. Up came a lorry loaded with horses destined for the chop! The horse was switched to that lorry and everyone drove off (that's horse trading!)

School had to be repaired and it looked like yet another squabble would ensue with the Borough Council. However, at the eleventh hour, all was resolved by some diplomatic work on my part at a planning meeting! It was very lucky that the church did not have to pay about four thousand pounds more for the windows to be leaded properly. The fear was that they would be smashed in the coming months by children playing football.

More recently, in 2005, the Rings Project caused a rift, but I can now say that this project will not be going ahead. I cannot help but wonder again: has the town missed out on something that could have made a difference? I was involved and, if the artist could have been pinned down to a final plan, perhaps we could have moved forward. However, by this time the new Community Centre was near to commencement and the fear was that the Rings would affect its viability. We were given a choice by our funders: the Community Centre, or the Rings! I think the right choice was made.

Feelings ran high once again when car parking charges were introduced in 2004 by West Devon Borough Council. Despite protests they went ahead. I expect we will have our squabbles again - it would not be a rural community if we didn't.

Watch this space!

LEISURE IN HATHERLEIGH

As the present trend is for health and sport to be connected, here might be a good place to mention the town's contribution to sport for the area. However, I was not good at sport!

The most common sports are Football, Cricket, Bowling, Tennis and Darts. These seem to have been the most strongly supported over the years. A few new sports have been played. It's sad to have witnessed, since the war, the demise of the rifle club, although shooting in the form of clays is now a very popular hobby. Throughout local history the men from Hatherleigh have always been keen shots. The firing range at Friars Hele has been there since the time that the rifle became popular, dating back to 1822. Colonel Pearse, the Queen's Prize man, used the range to acquire his skills. Traces of the firing butts can still be seen today.

On a visit in 2006 by the History Society it was discovered that, apart from some trees that have grown through the target mechanism, most of the range could be made to function again without major work. John Reynolds told us that he had found a weapon of some kind there in the last few years and the bomb disposal had blown it up where he had found it. Neither he nor they knew of its type.

In the mid 1980s, the cricket club constructed its present Pavilion and the club has progressed well, playing in one of the county's top leagues for a time. The pitch they play on today was purchased from the Balsdon family some time after the 1950s. Prior to that they played on the present football pitch in the sports field, which involved a lot of rolling - as you can imagine - just to get a reasonable surface.

Rugby does not seem to have taken off in the town but I am told that a rugby team did exist before my time.

CRICKET

The cricket club celebrated its centenary some years ago. My first memory at school was of playing cricket on the present football pitch and the Hatherleigh team used this as well. They purchased the present pitch from the Balsdon family who themselves have had at least three generations play. It is very likely that there will be a fourth. Over the years the team have had their ups and downs but the standard of cricket for the size of town has always been high and credit must be given to the club members for the work done over the years to build the Pavilion. This was opened by local radio celebrity, Ian Brass

President's Eleven: Len Jones (the President) left, bottom row.

BOWLING

The club celebrated its centenary in 1988 and, over the years, has produced several county players. The old club house can be seen in the first picture of the construction of the Bypass

A person that must be mentioned is Eric Rowe, who appears many times elsewhere in this book. He is a man dedicated to the town's sport clubs. My brother in-law, Tony Squires, is the President at the time of writing. He and my sister joined the club a few years ago; they were disappointed that the Skittle season had ended and I suggested they try bowling. They are now stalwart supporters, as are many others from outlying villages.

Many years ago the bowling green was at the top of the church cemetery. In the same area Cock Fighting was held in the distant days when it was legal.

Back row: G Down, J Thornbury, E Ball, D Guard, G Horn, D Bryant, J White. Front row: E Rowe, C Knight, J Knight, B Horn, E Bryant, E Sanders, G Bryant, C Weekes, J Weekes, J Sanders

E Rowe, D Knight, C Weeks

SCOUTING

Hatherleigh had one of the first Boy Scout groupa in Devon - hence the title 'The First Devon Scouts'. Wally Gooding, my father-in-law, was the Scout Master for many years and I have had access to photos from his collection, one of which is shown here. There are more on the next page too, including one of a gentleman with a clay

HATHERLEIGH TRIVIA - 12

GHOSTS!

Hatherleigh is not without ghost stories. Some of the houses that have had sightings include 27 High Street, 4 High Street and the shop No 2 in Market Street. There have also been sightings at Passaford House and Totleigh Barton. Most seem to have involved old ladies, leaning over the bed or coming through the wall and crossing the room. But in 27 High Street something brushes past you on the stairs and the sound of bells cross the floor of the bedroom. Passaford has involved a number of things, including footsteps and doors opening when only one person was there.

THE SALMON AND THE COPPER (NAMES HAVE BEEN CHANGED!)

A poacher was walking home one dark evening with a salmon tucked under his coat. He met the local Police Constable at the bottom of South Street "Hello George," says the Constable, "Going my way? Let me walk up South Street with you!" Struggling, the poacher held tight to his catch to keep it hidden. At the top of South Street they parted company. George said: "'Night Constable." "'Night George," the Constable replied, "I'll be up later when I finish my beat to have a piece of that salmon you have under your coat!"

THE DONKEY CART

New Road, the road in front of the Fire Station which has now been superceded by the Bypass, was about to be opened. The dignitaries were waiting and the ceremony was about to take place, with a ribbon to be cut. Around the corner came a well-known figure who always drove a donkey cart. He trotted straight through the ribbon and out onto the road laughing and chuckling.

HAVE I EVER BEEN SCARED?

Three times stand out in my memory. The first fire I attended - at Friars Hele - lightning was striking the ground all around the house and I was standing on the roof! I had never seen a house on fire before and here I was on the roof fighting the fire in the worst storm I have ever seen then, or since (storms were just as bad 50 years ago). Next, in Queenstown on New Zealand South Island, I wondered if I would return when the clouds came down over the Richardson Mountains when I was in a light aircraft flying to Milford Sound. We were lost,

flying in a 'tunnel' with a blanket of cloud overhead and massive mountains on either side. I kept the camera running as evidence if we did not come out of it! Finally, the day following - at Skippers Canyon - the road there is hacked out of the side of the mountain (see picture) and I drove down it not knowing it was so bad. My wife Lesley jumped out at the start and refused to go further. It's a drive I would not attempt again!

pipe. He often appears in photos. He's in the picture left too - third from left, back row, holding his pipe once again - and we have a definitive identification of him from another picture held by the History Society. His name is Mr. Burg. My theory is that he formed the first ever Scout Group, in Hatherleigh. Here's why.

The start of Scouting was about this time. Mr. Burg lived in Oslo House (he came from Norway) and he was the Chemist, a Dentist, a Photographer and many other things too - a man ahead of his time! It seems very possible to me that he could have been responsible for helping to start the Scouting movement. My father-in-law always said the Hatherleigh troop was the first in Devon (but I know other towns claim to have been the first also.) Nevertheless, we had high ranking Army officers in the area, with connections no doubt to Baden Powell, so I feel my theory should be pursued.

In the late 1940s, Hatherleigh First had a Scout Band and some of the players went on to play in the present Silver Band.

Mr Burg, with clay pipe. Did he help form the first ever Scout Group, in Hatherleigh?

FOOTBALL

The footballer, Alec Dickson, once visited the town with Tom Gooding. Alec played for Derby County and later became a godfather to Tom's daughter. Eric Rowe, who gave me a photo, did not know who he was and, when I told him, said: "I am not surprised. I had not seen a player like him in the team before. We won that day!"

Although I did not shine at football, I have always been very interested and, just recently, the club has made moves to purchase the pitch from the sports field committee to give them the opportunity to improve their facilities. Now, when you drive past the pitch, improvements are already visible, the biggest being the removal of the high hedge, and the smart railing surrounding the ground.

For the size of the town the club has always played at a very high standard. The pitch is the envy of larger clubs.

I once attended a Borough Council meeting at Okehampton and the football manager for their club at that time said that the pitch at Hatherleigh was too good for a small town: "It should be ours!" He was unaware that I came from Hatherleigh!

HAFC. (Back row) A Dickson, E Rowe, L Jones, C Smale, S Babb, J Hocking, T Gooding. (Front row) L Willis, H Searle, B Madge, G Gloyn.

DARTS

The Lane Darts League was started at Iddesleigh and named after Sir Alan Lane of the Penguin book empire. He was a frequent visitor to the Duke of York Inn at Iddesleigh, as was Sheila Van Dam the daughter of Mr. Vivian Van Dam from the Windmill Theatre in London.

They both became involved and the Duke of York became the headquarters of the League, covering many of the surrounding villages. The area around Hatherleigh has always been able to supply a stream of good darts players. There was always strong competition at the end of the season finals, which were often held in the local village hall because the pub would overflow.

The winning Darts team from a mid 1960s Lane Darts League Final. (Back Row) W Jones, E Rowe, R Meardon ,D Weeks, E Orchard, L Cole, C White (killed in a car crash shortly after this picture was taken). (Front Row) W Anstey, R Vallance, S Netherway, W Casser.

When Hatherleigh had four Public Houses they would all supply a team to the League. Sir Alan Lane's daughter, Clara, and her husband Michael Murpurgo loved the area so much that they have settled in Iddesleigh, starting the 'Farms For City Children' project at Nethercott House. A very proud moment for Michael was when he was awarded the OBE in the 2006 Queen's Birthday Honours List for being a children's writer, with many books to his credit.

FLYING AT SHEEPWASH

I have always been interested in flying, and

joined the Royal Observer corps at the age of 16. One reason for joining, I must admit, is that you had a free flight once a year! Although I was petrified of warplanes in my childhood, my love of flying grew. I can say I have flown in most types of aircraft - helicopters, gliders, hot air balloons, airliners, RAF transports and microlights. I have also been paragliding.

Aerial view of one of the fly-ins. Note the number of aircraft on the ground - see also below (1989/1990).

When the opportunity came to join the Sheepwash Flying club, I jumped at the chance. The club was started by Charlie Trace, a local farmer who learnt to fly in the Second World War. During the sixties he found flying light aircraft was within his budget and bought a small plane, flying out of one of his own fields at Sheepwash. Over the years many visitors have come down especially for this event and stayed at the Half Moon Inn. Among them were ex RAF and airport support staff who liked what they saw. Some came to live or buy second homes. They socialised in the Half Moon Inn and eventually the landlords (The Innis family), locals and Charlie formed the Sheepwash Flying Club. The fly-ins which were organised once a year were very popular until Charlie's health forced him to stop flying.

This led to the demise of the club. I wonder, if they had continued, what Health and Safety would have made of the event. Spectators were able to get close to the aircraft. These days things would have had to change. It has been a great loss to many of the frustrated flyers in the area, myself included.

THE WALRUSES

The Walruses are a charity group formed at the Tally Ho by Gianni Scosse, the landlord in 1986. The idea was to have a sponsored dip in the River Lew on New Years Day, staying in for five minutes to raise money for charity by sponsorship. Twenty years later they've managed to raise £30,000, and they are not planning to stop At the turn of this century they had their most risky event due

The 2007 Walrus dip, which celebrated 20 years of fund raising.

HATHERLEIGH TRIVIA - 13

THE BODY

The body of a lady was found in the River Lew in the early 1970s. On a summer's evening a fisherman near the old Railway Station came across what he thought was a tailor's dummy in the overhanging branches, just above the water line. On closer examination he realised it was a body that had been there for some months. He informed the police. Rumour spread around the town. It turned out that the lady came from a house at Moor View. Her husband had thought she had left him and gone to live elsewhere. After an inquest it turned out that she had been washed down after a flood from Hanaborough Brook. The cause of death was not identified but she had a broken leg and, as she was known to use the area for walks, an open verdict was passed.

A POSTMAN'S LIFE!

During my 19 years as a postman I found you could help many people many times - but make one mistake and you were given no quarter! On one occasion mail had been delivered to the wrong address on the other side of the town by another postman (the address was confusing admittedly!) and, despite me pleading that it was not my fault, the householder would not understand, so it was me who caught her wrath. Any help which I had given her in the past did not count. Most letter boxes are inadequate too, and are always in contention. We would often get letters with an address like - 'the Pink House in Bridge Street'. One favourite was: 'the house where the (person's name) lives'!

One incident I remember clearly. This time the lady concerned gave me high praise. I had to deliver a letter addressed to: 'the person that sat by me last night at the Japanese prisoners' reunion in Plymouth'. I knew one of the families on my round was Dutch and I remembered that many Dutch had been taken prisoner in Singapore. I worked out that the husband would be about the right age so I put the letter in their box.

The next day the lady asked: "how did you know that letter was for me?" She said it was she who had been the prisoner, not her husband, and that she had been taken as a child of 9. She went on to tell me the story of how children were treated in those times, and how those fathered by Japanese soldiers were treated especially well while the rest were treated badly.

to heavy rainfall during the hour preceding the start. The water rose a foot or more in a short time and continued to rise whilst they were dipping. In the opinion of some, a tragedy was only just avoided. However, £3,300 was raised for the new Community Centre. In 2006, a DVD was made of all the Walrus dips in the river, taken from the hours of video recordings that I made over the previous 20 years.

The Walruses, taken the year that the bypass was being built when the dip took place south of the bridge. Alan Jones is in the foreground.

THE RUBY RUN

In 2003, I was the Hatherleigh Town Mayor. It had intrigued me for years that Hatherleigh and Holsworthy were a half marathon - i.e. 13.3 miles - apart. At the Holsworthy 'Pretty Maid' ceremony I suggested to Richard Brown, the Mayor of Holsworthy at that time, that a half marathon should be run between our two towns. He agreed.

Finishing in Holsworthy Square, 10th June 2007.

We alternate the direction of the course each year and, with the help of a dedicated committee, we have just held our 5th race. The two Town Councils and many of the two town's inhabitants have helped make this event a great success. The 2007 race attracted over three hundred runners and walkers. The event has raised more than £15,000 for charity since it started.

SUSTRANDS

This National Group is developing cycle routes throughout Europe. Their aim is to create a route from Gibraltar through Spain to Aberdeen, passing through Hatherleigh and the Tarka trail, then west into North Cornwall. It's already in place from Meeth to Lynton. The Hatherleigh to Meeth section should be ready by 2009. As Mayor of West Devon in 1998, I cycled to raise funds for the Mayor's charity and to protest at the small amount of government grants for rural areas. My journey of 365 miles took one week and stretched from Cirencester to Plymouth. I raised £560 for the NSPCC.

THE SILVER BAND

Lastly in this Leisure chapter, I would like to pay tribute to the Hatherleigh Silver Band, which is one of Hatherleigh's finest assets. What can be said about this well-known outfit?

The Silver Band goes back over 100 years, as you can see from the picture on the left. Sanders, Vallance and Pillivant/Wonnacott are just some of the names which have contributed to the Band's history.

Praise must go to the band leaders for the work they do with young people - many not from Hatherleigh - who go on to play in the main band. Many band members are from families that have supported the band for years. Outdoor events in the area often invite the Silver Band to give that lovely musical touch - and how welcome it is.

The Silver Band has won many awards, and has competed in national events at Wembley and Bristol. They have also cut a couple of CDs - which have been played on local radio - and they have been seen at many televised events.

Long may they continue to play!

FINAL THOUGHTS

The area around Hatherleigh has always relied on farming and this has presented a big challenge since the 1990s. Many thought farming could not get any worse. Now, the many restrictions and increased red tape that have been introduced in the last 15 to 20 years mean that, in 2007, the farming industry is undergoing greater change than at any time since I started researching this book. More and more farmers are going out of business every day.

When I started to write in 1995, many farmers would not have dreamt that they would have been in the position they are today. What does this mean for the town in this new century? I wonder if the cattle market can keep going. There are so many threats to the country's sparse rural areas, such as buying and selling on the Internet, and the large supermarkets are having a huge effect on local shops, which simply cannot compete. I don't expect Devon farming will ever return to the days of the 1980's, although history does has a habit of going full circle!

With the Sustrands Cycle route passing through the town, we see more cyclists every day and that is bound to be a boost for tourism. Whether this will have enough impact to push us forward sufficiently I doubt very much. For three years the BBC have broadcast 'Springwatch' live from Fishleigh Farm Estate. It is watched by millions of viewers but Hatherleigh has not had a mention despite my many efforts. We seem to have lost another opportunity which I am sure would have boosted green tourism for our area. I have high hopes someday that a project will be put forward from the Fishleigh Estate that will be a flagship for the area.

The Co-op shop has recently had a complete overhaul. This main food shop for the town has gone through many ownerships, from Vivianne's store situated at the junction of High Street and Bridge Street to the International Stores. It then moved to the Market entrance and became Somerfield's, and then Spar, then Alldays convenience store and finally the Co-op. It is now thriving, and we are all pleased at the way this is now bringing more people in from outlying areas to shop.

It had always been a plan to have another school entrance and I am working on that now. Will it come to fruition? Nothing is certain, although things look optimistic.

I loved geography lessons at school and we were taught about many parts of the world in the 1940s and 1950s. Travel was not as it is today. I never thought then that I would have the opportunity to travel to far flung places. Up until 1972 I had never left the shores of the UK but, gradually, travel became cheaper and much easier. Since then I have visited many parts of the world.

I recommend, to all the young people who may read this, to travel the world as much as you can. I have had the fortune to visit many of the world's cities including New York, San Francisco, Paris, Brussels, Amsterdam, Bonn, Sidney, Perth, Wellington, Auckland, Rome, Pompeii, Marrakech, Singapore, Hong Kong, Moscow, Fiji and Yekaterinberg. There are many, many more to visit.

Most interesting to me is that I have seen some of the things and places that we were taught about in geography all those years ago by John Wilcox, a teacher who brought them to life even though he probably never visited them. He even told us about farming methods that are still being used 50 years later. There is so much to see and learn. The planet Earth is a wonderful place.

Many residents of Hatherleigh, both past and present, have also had an influence on me - giving advice and telling stories. I have always listened to them and it has been a pleasure. One person who stands out was my father-in-law Wally Gooding. He had a tremendous influence on me. I respected him and missed him terribly when he suddenly died. He would have been tickled pink to find that I have mentioned him, and displayed his photo in this book, standing by the last train in Hatherleigh.

Now, as I finish this book, I find it is very satisfying that, since I married and moved to Hatherleigh, I have taken a very active part in the town. I am proud to have been the Town Mayor so many times. It was also a great honour in 1998, when I became Mayor of West Devon Borough Council for the first time, and then again in 2007.

Whilst I have been representing Hatherleigh and the surrounding areas I have been able to help guide a way forward. But I think that, over the years, having served on so many committees, services and organisations, my family life has paid a price. Lesley and the children often had to stay at home when I was on weekend duty for the Fire Brigade. She had to cover for me in the Fish and Chip shop on many occasions.

She always gave me so much support ... but now I can never tell her how much I appreciated it.

Looking back, I realise how lucky I have been to have had a wonderful, understanding family. Many of the things I have achieved should be shared with them. I sometimes feel guilty that, perhaps, I have achieved my ambitions and objectives at the expense of others.

As I write these last few words and place my final jigsaw piece into the picture of my 67 years on this planet, I wonder what someone else - 67 years on in 2075 - might write as a sequel. If this planet is still hurtling through space, what will Hatherleigh - and the world I have seen - be like?

I also wonder what kind of media will be used to record it!

Thanks for reading my book.

Dennis

A WORKING MAN'S LIFE

In Devon, flexibility can be the key to survival. Here's my CV! Anyone interested in employing a labouring rent collector who can build houses, deliver letters, fry, film, drive lorries and be Mayor should definitely not call me! Haven't I done enough already?

One Tuesday, during that period in the 1990s when I had 7 jobs, I started with the post round at 6am then went to the Market to collect rents at 9.30am. At 11.30am I completed a short piece of filming for a client then, at 12.30pm, I attended a short Council meeting at Okehampton that went on until 1.30pm. I came home, attended a fire with the Fire Brigade for a short time and in the evening fried in the Fish and Chip shop!

I ended my day at 10.00pm, knackered!

Year	Job 1	Job 2	Job 3	Job 4	Job 5	Job 6	Job 7
1955	Farm Labourer						
1961	Lorry Driver						
1965	Builder	Farm Labourer					
1967		Fireman					
1972			Fish and Chips				
1974				Postman			
1977					Market (Various)	Videoing Weddings	
1991							West Devon Councillor
1995							
1998		Mayor					
2004							
2005	Property Developer						
2007		Mayor					
2008							
?	?	?	?	?	?	?	?